Start Your Own

WEDDING CONSULTANT BUSINESS

7 Day Loan

Additional titles in *Entrepreneur's* **Startup Series**

Start Your Own

Bar or Club

Bed & Breakfast

Business on eBay

Business Support Service

Car Wash

Child Care Service

Cleaning Service

Clothing Store

Coin-Operated Laundry

Consulting

Crafts Business

e-Business

e-Learning Business

Event Planning Business

Executive Recruiting Service

Freight Brokerage Business

Gift Basket Service

Growing and Selling Herbs and Herbal
   Products

Home Inspection Service

Import/Export Business

Information Consultant Business

Law Practice

Lawn Care or Landscaping Business

Mail Order Business

Medical Claims Billing Service

Personal Concierge Service

Personal Training Business

Pet-Sitting Business

Restaurant and Five Other Food Businesses

Self-Publishing Business

Seminar Production Business

Specialty Travel & Tour Business

Staffing Service

Successful Retail Business

Vending Business

Wholesale Distribution Business

Entrepreneur
MAGAZINE'S

startup

2ND EDITION

Start Your Own

WEDDING CONSULTANT BUSINESS

*Your Step-by-Step
Guide to Success*

Entrepreneur Press and Amy Jean Peters

EP
Entrepreneur.
Press

Editorial Director: Jere L. Calmes
Managing Editor: Marla Markman
Cover Design: Beth Hansen-Winter
Production and Composition: Eliot House Productions

This publication is designed to provide accurate and authoritative information in regard to the subject matter covered. It is sold with the understanding that the publisher is not engaged in rendering legal, accounting or other professional services. If legal advice or other expert assistance is required, the services of a competent professional person should be sought.

Library of Congress Cataloging-in-Publication Data

Peters, Amy Jean.
    Start your own wedding consultant business/by Entrepreneur Press and Amy Jean Peters.—2nd ed.
        p.   cm.
    Rev. ed. of: Start your own wedding consultant business/Eileen Figure Sandlin. 2003
    Includes index.
    ISBN-13: 978-1-59918-102-8 (alk. paper)
    ISBN-10: 1-59918-102-9 (alk. paper)
    1. Wedding supplies and services industry—Management. 2. Consulting firms—Management. 3. New business enterprises—Management. I. Sandlin, Eileen Figure. Start your own wedding consultant business. II. Entrepreneur Press. III. Title.
HD9999.W372S26 2007
392.5068'1—dc22   2007011671

Printed in Canada
12 11 10 09 08   10 9 8 7 6 5 4 3 2

Contents

▲

Chapter 13

Learning from Your Experience 133

Appendix

Wedding Consultant Resources. 143

Preface to the Revised Edition

Since the first edition of *Start Your Own Wedding Consultant Business* was published in 2003, there have been dramatic and exciting changes in the wedding consultant field. In fact, if you are considering a career in this dynamic area, the stars are perfectly aligned for your launch.

Perhaps, most marked is the percentage of couples who decide to hire a consultant to make their big day picture perfect in every imaginable way. Two-thirds of brides- and grooms-to-be opt to work with a consultant. Of those who choose not to use a consultant, an amazing 72 percent wish they had, finding out too late that they simply could not handle the myriad details involved in creating the wedding of their dreams.

In fact, many reception sites are requiring that couples hire and work with a consultant. In particular, in a growing number of urban areas the majority of reception sites absolutely mandate that a wedding consultant be involved in the planning and design. Additionally, many wedding vendors are beginning to offer discounts to brides and grooms who work with wedding consultants because these weddings tend to run more smoothly, causing fewer headaches for the vendors.

Consider, too, that a recent CNN report suggests that within five years wedding consultants will be considered standard service providers at all weddings, just as caterers and photographers are now considered *de rigeuer*.

Today's couples, because they are marrying later in life, are often full-time workers, engaged with challenging careers and managing homes. Planning a wedding takes hundreds of hours, time these couples simply don't have available to devote to their wedding plans.

As Deborah McCoy, President of American Academy of Wedding Professionals, says, "People are funny when it comes to a wedding; it's such a fantasy. They think, 'nothing can happen to me.' They're very naïve. If you were going to pay $27,000 for a car, for example (often given as the average cost of a wedding), you would do your due diligence; you would become an educated consumer. Couples today don't have time to become educated and do the proper due diligence, so they hire a wedding consultant to do it for them."

This new edition of *Start Your Own Wedding Consultant Business* takes a fresh and updated look at the burgeoning field of wedding consulting. It offers scores of updated facts, figures, tips, contacts, and advice covering everything from the most-requested catering "in's"—small bites are in, super size food is out—to shining a spotlight on the trends brides are following to make their special day one-of-a-kind. This guide also offers updated information on the "nuts-and-bolts" issues of setting up your new business including creating a business plan, writing a powerful mission statement, finding an ideal site from which to do business, buying adequate liability insurance, developing a pipeline of reliable vendors, marketing your business, learning how to network with amazing results, using blogs to keep abreast of the most up-to-the-minute wedding news and trends, and more.

Sincere thanks to the many wedding consultants and other wedding professionals who gave generously of their time to help in creating this guide. Hats off to Leslie Bullock, Robbi Ernst III, Kathie Flood, Chris Graze, Lisa Kronauer, Deborah McCoy, Ann Nola, Kim Roberts, and Nancy Tucker for their good spirit and sage advice.

Here Comes the Bride ...

and the Wedding Consultant

Many newly wed brides have cautionary tales to tell: about the flowers that didn't arrive, the tuxedoes that didn't fit, the limo that ran late, or the caterer that forgot the sauce for the chicken. These brides all share a common bond: they did not choose to hire a wedding consultant.

When asked what one thing these brides would change if they had the big day to do again, the majority agree that they would hire a wedding consultant.

In fact, wedding consultants are becoming much like the photographer, a required rather than optional element in every bride and groom's planning process. Increasingly, venues are requiring that couples hire a consultant to ensure that their special day goes off without any hitches.

Who Should Hire a Wedding Consultant

For many couples, hiring a consultant is an essential part of the planning process. According to an Economic Policy Institute Study, working women put in a remarkable 46 hours on the job every week. Add to this the fact that 60 percent of women ages 16 and up are in the work force, up from 20 percent at the turn of the century. These numbers reveal that brides-to-be simply don't have the hours needed to plan a wedding. Women are often too busy juggling the demands of their professional and personal lives to oversee the details necessary to create the wedding of their dreams.

This has created an enormous opportunity for anyone considering a career as a wedding consultant. As Deborah McCoy, president of American Academy of Wedding Professionals™, explains, "Everyone is the audience for wedding consultants. Couples are marrying later in life, after their educations are completed and their careers are established. How can you run a house, have a career, and plan weddings? You can't—and that's why wedding consultants are so essential for brides- and grooms-to-be."

Although it is difficult to pinpoint an exact figure for how many wedding consultant businesses there are nationwide, the best guess is approximately 10,000, according to Gerard Monaghan, president of the Association of Bridal Consultants (ABC). Monaghan says that although no one formally tracks these figures, his estimate is based on the number of people who pay for memberships to the various professional associations, as well as the number of people on mailing lists available from list brokers.

Billion Dollar Business

Weddings are very big business in the United States. The Fairchild Bridal Group estimates that in 2006, as much as $125 billion in indirect billing could be spent on 2.1 million weddings. Part of the reason for the propensity to spend big bucks on a dream wedding is that there are often six wage earners funding the event: the bridal couple themselves, and the bride and groom's parents. This has driven the cost of the average wedding up over the years. The Fairchild Bridal Group puts the average cost of a wedding at $30,000, a 73 percent increase over the past 15 years. Another wedding research group, onewed.com, puts the average cost at $25,000. Wedding costs

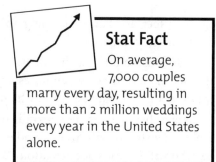

Stat Fact

On average, 7,000 couples marry every day, resulting in more than 2 million weddings every year in the United States alone.

vary, of course, depending on their location. A wedding in Fargo won't set the couple back as much as a wedding fete in New York City where incomes are higher and services more expensive. Ann Nola, director of the Association of Certified Professional Wedding Consultants, puts the average cost of a California wedding at $40,000, a full $10,000 to $15,000 higher than in many parts of the country.

All of these indictors point to the bridal consultant field as a burgeoning and rapidly expanding field. This industry outlook sets the stage for success for both new and established wedding consultants. According to Robbi Ernst III, president of June Wedding, Inc., a novice consultant who coordinates ten weddings a year and charges the industry's standard fee of 10 to 15 percent per event can expect to gross $17,500 to $26,250 in sales. A more experienced consultant who handles 40 weddings a year can earn $70,000 and up.

"The earnings potential for wedding consultants is awesome," says Richard Markel of the Association for Wedding Professionals International. "Those who are better connected and better educated will do the best in this business, as will those who network as a way to build their reputations."

What It Takes to Be a Wedding Consultant

So what does it take to be a successful wedding consultant? Loreen C., who owns a wedding consultant business in Ypsilanti, Michigan, says emphatically, "A sense of humor." And she's not kidding.

Adds Lisa K., a wedding consultant in Connecticut, "you have to be willing and ready to jump through hoops. It's fun but it is challenging."

As a wedding consultant, you will be depending on the professionalism and reliability of up to a dozen or more people to create a bride's dream wedding. When dealing with so many vendors, there's always the possibility that something will go askew or bomb out completely. That's why having a sense of humor and the ability to think on your feet are key to keeping things on track or fixing the problems that will inevitably crop up.

"I do laugh a lot, but that doesn't mean I'm taking anything lightly," Loreen says. "I'll put my foot down when necessary. But being warm and friendly puts clients who are tired and frustrated at ease, which makes my job easier."

In fact, being a people person is pretty much a requirement for this job. You'll be dealing constantly with weepy brides, demanding mothers, cranky suppliers, and others who will vie for your attention. You'll be bargaining with vendors, overseeing the

An Eye for Trends

The wedding business is always changing as couples keep pushing the nuptial envelope, looking for imaginative ways in which to make their wedding special, unique, and memorable. A successful wedding consultant should have the ability to keep an eye on trends as they develop—and as they fade. Ann Nola of the Association of Certified Professional Wedding Consultants gives these current wedding "in's:"

○ Private estates as wedding and reception sites
○ Smaller wedding size as brides and grooms trim their lists, focusing on family, close friends, and longtime co-workers.
○ A return to formality.
○ Whimsical and colorful invitations.
○ Clever "save the date" reminders such as refrigerator magnets
○ Theme-oriented weddings
○ Monogram-themed weddings—everything from the invitations to the menus are adorned with the couple's monogram,
○ Small bridal parties
○ Elegant bridal gowns as well as adding subtle color to the bride's gown.
○ Tuxedoes styled in a more suit-like fashion.
○ Table names instead of table numbers, for instance the tables might be named after a couple's favorite spots or favorite sports.
○ A trend toward personalization.

Nola is based in California so some of her trend-spotting may not apply to your area. However, she demonstrates through her keen observation the ability to stay on top of hot trends. Successful wedding planners will need to do the same in their locales.

activities of hordes of hired helpers, and mingling with the guests at wedding receptions. So it helps if you really love working with people and have an upbeat, positive outlook that will help you weather the inevitable problems that can arise when you're coordinating countless details.

Nancy Tucker, owner of Coordinators' Corner, puts it this way, "There are so many skills needed for a wedding consultant but above all they must be personable. They have the task of first selling the need for a wedding consultant and then selling themselves as they right one for the job."

On the more practical side, it also helps to have a strong business background. While it's not impossible to make a go of a wedding consultant business if you've never balanced a checkbook, previous experience with handling finances (even household budgets) as well as managing day-to-day office details is certainly valuable. After all, you will be coordinating budgets and overseeing finances for your clients. Plus you'll be taking care of the details of running your own business, which will include taxes, billing, and other financial matters. You may even have to deal with personnel administration at some point in your career. So business experience—or barring that, at least a good head for numbers and details—is critical to your success.

Robbi Ernst III, founder and president of June Wedding Inc, feels strongly about having this all-important business sense and education. "Ideally, if a person is going to be able to grow his company, he must have an education in basic business... management, marketing, attainment of goals, creation and maintenance of spreadsheets, and accounting."

"An entrepreneurial spirit is also very important," says Julia K., who runs a successful wedding consultant business in a suburb of Dallas. "You have to be able to identify what's good for the business and what isn't, then make the appropriate moves."

The Benefits of Consulting

There are many challenges in this business, to be sure, but along with these challenges come great rewards. Assuming there's no shotgun involved, you are always working with happy (though understandably nervous) people. You are the catalyst that makes the biggest moment of their lives special and memorable. And you can have the satisfaction of seeing all the details you have so painstakingly planned come together seamlessly and effectively.

"The end result is definitely the best part," says Loreen, the wedding consultant in Ypsilanti, Michigan. "All I do is eat, sleep, and dream weddings, but it's worth it because it's so much fun."

In addition to the satisfaction of being able to make dream weddings come true for your clients, there's another really appealing reason for embarking on a career in

Do You Have the Right Stuff?

Take this short quiz to see if you have what it takes to become a successful wedding consultant:

1. Can you juggle a variety of tasks at various stages of development all at the same time?

   ❏Yes   ❏No

2. Are you detail oriented?

   ❏Yes   ❏No

3. Are you self-motivated and able to work without direct supervision?

   ❏Yes   ❏No

4. Are your calendar and other important papers within reach rather than hopelessly buried under piles of office detritus?

   ❏Yes   ❏No

5. Are you disciplined enough to work even when the birds are singing, it's sunny and warm outside, and the house needs painting?

   ❏Yes   ❏No

6. Are you comfortable working alone without the benefit of chattering co-workers, coffee klatches, and holiday parties?

   ❏Yes   ❏No

7. Can you handle emotionally fragile brides, demanding mothers, and irritable suppliers without succumbing to the urge to deck them?

   ❏Yes   ❏No

8. Can you say "no" and mean it?

   ❏Yes   ❏No

9. Can you laugh genteelly when things go wrong, then think fast on your feet to fix them?

   ❏Yes   ❏No

10. Can you lead a conga line and do the Macarena when called upon?

   ❏Yes   ❏No

Add up your "yes" answers. Scoring:

8 to 10 = Congratulations! You have the makings of an excellent wedding consultant.

4 to 7 = With some hard work, you can go a long way in this field.

1 to 3 = Thank goodness you bought this book.

0 = Maybe you should try a career in trucking or construction!

wedding consulting: You become the proud chief executive officer of your own small business. As such, you answer to no one, except maybe the IRS. You can do things your own way. You can set up shop in a spare bedroom or opt for a commercial space. You can set your own hours and make your own schedule. You can take on as much or as little work as you wish. Not that you'll have lots of free time for lazy days on the beach in Maui or strolls down the Champs Elysées. Wedding consulting is hard work. You'll have a mind-boggling number of details to coordinate, oodles of suppliers to baby-sit, long days shifting from one achy foot to the other, and legions of anxious brides (not to mention their mothers) to reassure and soothe.

Does this sound like fun to you, too? Great! Then you have come to the right place. The guide you're holding in your hands will show you how to start a wedding consulting business. We'll cover day-to-day responsibilities and the various tasks integral to running this type of business. We'll also touch on the myriad issues a new business owner will face, such as taxes, insurance, and financing issues. But perhaps best of all, you'll find that this guide is punctuated with advice and words of wisdom from successful wedding consultants who have turned their personal dreams of working in an industry they love into reality. You can do it, too! So turn the page, and let's get started making dreams come true.

The Basics of
Wedding
Consulting

For pomp, circumstance, and sheer drama, there are few events in life that can equal that of a carefully planned wedding. From the solemn ceremony to an elegant country club reception, dresses with yards and yards of pristine white peau de soie and tulle, debonair tuxedoes, and sleek stretch limousines, weddings are as much a staged production as the

Wedding News

August is the top wedding month with 10.2 percent of brides and grooms choosing this sultry month to tie the knot. June, traditionally considered the reigning matrimonial month, comes in a close second with 9.9 percent of couples choosing this summer month to take their vows.

most elaborate Broadway show. Even if the nuptials are more intimate and the budget more modest, weddings still require a great deal of advanced planning and follow-up to make sure every element of this momentous day comes together as planned—on time and within budget.

In the past, wedding planning activities were often relegated to the mother of the bride or another female family member who had an eye for fashion and a flair for floral design. There was a strict code of appropriate behavior and proper etiquette that dictated exactly how the bridal party should dress and interact.

All has changed with the influx of women into the workplace over the past 30 years. With 60 percent of women in the workplace, today's mother of the bride is probably a working woman herself who does not have any more time to attend to details such as limousine rentals or reception hall contracts than the bride herself does. This has opened up a world of opportunity for well-organized, enthusiastic consultants. Professional wedding consultants treat their vocation as a business, not as a pleasant hobby or sideline.

Deborah McCoy, president of American Academy of Wedding Professionals, emphasizes this point. "Education, training, and experience are needed to become a wedding consultant. That's paramount. You cannot plan one wedding, your own, for example, and think that you're a competent wedding planner. You don't take chances with a day that can't be replicated."

"Today's consultants are men and women trained in the administrative and legal affairs of their industry," adds Robbi Ernst, founder and president of June Wedding Inc. "They are the team leaders who orchestrate the entire wedding, including the wedding day itself."

The Role of the Consultant

Toward that end, many wedding consultants routinely serve as event planners, budget watchdogs, etiquette experts, troubleshooters, and on-site supervisors. They accompany brides-to-be to appointments for fittings, floral consultations, and other services. They provide a shoulder to cry on and a sympathetic ear for stressed-out clients. They also act as creative problem-solvers who can quickly assess a situation

Words from the Wise

Robbi Ernst of June Wedding Inc. offers these sage words of advice to anyone contemplating a career as a wedding consultant:

○ Seek out the best and most competent professional training in the wedding industry. "Go to the experts and let them teach you not to make the mistakes they made. This can save you a small fortune," Ernst says.

○ Take business and computer courses, including classes on marketing, at your local community college.

○ If possible, work for a well-known consultant for a while as an apprentice.

○ Have enough funds to carry you through three years, since it will take that long before you see a profit.

○ Decide whether you are going to do this as a hobby or as a career. "If you don't make this decision early on, you're going to be frustrated and unhappy," Ernst says.

and devise a viable solution—often without anyone in the bridal party ever knowing a potential disaster has been averted.

Some wedding consultants prefer to offer consulting services only, and may provide a comprehensive "wedding blueprint" package that consists of realistic budgets, detailed schedules, and lists of reliable vendors. Still others provide insight and assistance with the social etiquette part of the wedding experience.

The scope of your own involvement is entirely up to you. The trend in the industry, however, has been toward offering total coordination of the entire blessed event because, as noted earlier, brides and their mothers just don't have time to attend to the mountain of details necessary to pull off the wedding they dream of. That means you must have an in-depth knowledge of every aspect of wedding planning and know how to make all the details mesh smoothly and effectively.

Business Basics

Let's start with some administrative basics. No matter where you decide to conduct the majority of your business, or what your personal management style may be, there are certain tasks that are common to all wedding consultants. Among them are day-to-day business administration, bridal consultations, and vendor and service coordination. Here's a look at each of these activities.

A Day in the Life

Even though no two days tend to be alike for wedding consultants because the tastes and needs of their clients vary so widely, there are certain tasks you can expect to do on a regular basis. To begin with, you'll spend lots of time on the telephone every day, fielding inquiries from interested brides, following up on vendor leads, and checking on the status of wedding preparations. If you employ contract or temporary help during weddings, you'll have to meet with them on a regular basis to provide instructions and go over details. You will also spend a significant amount of time with the brides themselves, either conducting consultations or accompanying them to appointments with suppliers.

Then there is the paperwork. You'll have contracts to review, tax forms to file, and other business-related papers to shuffle. You will also have to keep meticulous records on the choices that your brides make, the status of wedding day plans, and other details. A word of advice: No matter how good your memory is, you should always jot down every appointment and activity. The number of details you will have to attend to as a wedding consultant will be truly mind-boggling, and when you're busy and short of time, it will be too easy for something to fall through the cracks—possibly with disastrous results. There is absolutely no substitute for good record keeping.

> **Tip...**
>
> **Smart Tip**
>
> Since you're going to spend a great deal of time on the phone every day, a telephone headset is a must. Not only does it give you hands-free freedom, but it also saves you from the neck strain that comes from cradling the receiver between your head and your shoulder. Also, a head set for your cell phone is an absolute must. Many states now require their use and issue tickets to those using hand-held cell phones.

The All Important Consultation

The first step in determining what a bride wants and how much she wants to turn over to you is to schedule a consultation. Don't even consider working with a bride- and groom-to-be until you've had this all important first meeting.

Ann Nola, director of the Association of Certified Professional Wedding Consultants, says that this point is critical. "It is just as important for the bride to know she can work with the wedding consultant as it is for the wedding consultant to know she can work with the bride. That is why having a consultation is absolutely essential. You have to see if the personalities match." Nola's company offers complimentary consultations because they are so vital to the success of the bride and groom's big day.

Other consultants charge a nominal fee—say, $50 per hour—for their time. In his book, *Great Wedding Tips from the Experts* (Lowell House), Robbi Ernst of June Wedding Inc. says, "A genuinely professional wedding consultant isn't going to talk with [anyone] for free, unless it is simply an introductory meeting . . . to determine if you are a good match for each other."

According to Ernst, the fee for a single consultation meeting typically ranges from $175 in smaller communities to as much as $500 in metropolitan areas. Charging a fee will help to cut down on the number of women who are just "shopping around" for services without making a commitment.

> **Tip...**
>
> ## Smart Tip
>
> As you develop your wedding consultant business, you will develop payment strategies for initial consultations. For some consultants, charging a nominal fee works—for others, like Ann Nola, offering a complimentary consultation helps her to find brides and grooms with whom she feels most compatible. As Nancy Tucker of Coordinators' Corner explains, "There are a wide range of fee arrangements for wedding consultants. Consultants find out what works best for their business."

On the other hand, Dolores E., a wedding consultant in Larkspur, California, offers a two-hour complimentary consultation for brides who wish to execute their own plans. She earns her fee by preparing a "blueprint" package for these brides, which provides a preferred vendor list, a detailed schedule, and ready-to-use budget spreadsheets. It takes her about two hours to prepare the package, and she charges a flat rate for the service.

One caveat: Avoid conducting casual consultations at your kitchen table or in your basement rec room. If you're going to see clients at home, usher them into a tidy, well-appointed office to reinforce your image as a competent professional. Also, plan on meeting with clients when children are at school or old enough to occupy themselves in another room. Keep pets in another room—even if the bride-to-be claims to love animals. Nothing will dampen her enthusiasm more than seeing a distracted consultant who is busy calming a crying baby or telling the dog to sit down and behave. You are a professional and need to always project a calm and in-charge posture.

During a consultation, it is important to determine exactly how much the bride wants you to do. Sometimes, she will prefer to do much of the groundwork herself (such as selecting a reception hall, ordering the cake and flowers, and auditioning the band or DJ), then will ask you to coordinate all the services and be on site during the reception. Other times, a busy bride will want to turn over all or many of these tasks to you, limiting her involvement to approving the choices presented to her and signing checks for the deposits.

For this reason, it's advisable to offer a variety of packages with varying levels of service. The idea is to provide choices that will allow the bride to customize her wedding to her exact specifications.

Suggested wedding packages might include:

- *Full-service package*: wedding planning and event supervision from beginning to end
- *Rehearsal and wedding day package*: on-site coordination and execution
- Wedding-day-only package: full or day supervision of wedding party festivities and vendors
- *Planning package*: budgets, spreadsheets, vendor recommendations, and other details
- *Party package*: planning and coordination of the engagement party, rehearsal dinner, and bachelor and bachelorette parties

Stat Fact

You probably can guess that Las Vegas is the wedding capital of the nation, with 100,000 weddings a year. That amounts to a whopping 300-plus weddings per day. But you may be surprised to know that Gatlinburg, Tennessee, is number two, with 42,000 nuptials, according to Richard Markel of the Association for Wedding Professionals International. This town, tucked into the heart of the Smoky Mountains is famed for its southern hospitality and special wedding packages for brides- and groom-to-be.

If the couple is reluctant to take on a consultant, at the very least, says Ann Nola, encourage the pair to sign on for the wedding-day-only package. "If then, along the way, the couple find themselves overwhelmed by the planning process—and most do—then they will call you to add other services."

Wedding Day Duties

All the wedding consultants we spoke to said they act as the bride's advocate on the happy day—running interference with suppliers, making sure the wedding party is dressed and where they're supposed to be on time, and so on. Some consultants, like Julia K. in Oak Point, Texas, and Packy B. in Broadview Heights, Ohio, prepare snacks and drinks for the wedding party to nibble on before the wedding so they don't go down the aisle with rumbling stomachs. To make sure all these tasks run like clockwork, most wedding planners create a detailed wedding day schedule that's provided to each member of the wedding party, the parents, and other relatives, as well as to the vendors who are responsible for providing various services.

Consultants often hire extra help on a contract basis to assist with wedding day activities. Their duties may range from greeting guests to taking care of the wedding party and families (refilling drinks, assisting the bride in the powder room, and so on). These contractors are hired on an as-needed basis and are paid either by the hour (around $10 to $15 per hour) or by the function ($100 to $150 per day).

Consulting Services and Fees

Charges for consulting services vary widely. Typically, consultants charge by the hour or by the package. Some consultants will charge up to 15 percent of the total wedding cost, but this is a more common practice in larger cities where disposable income is higher and there are more top-level female executives footing the bill.

According to Robbi Ernst of June Wedding, Inc., preparation-planning fees, which include everything except wedding day coordination, usually range between $2,000 and $4,500, depending on whether your business is in a rural or metropolitan area. Full production coordination, which includes everything from early planning and budgeting to wedding day activity coordination, will cost an additional $1,500 to $3,000 on average. A wedding that's very large or complex may cost much more.

According to the wedding consultants interviewed for this book, full production package rates ranged from $1,000 to $5,000. The higher prices were found in the largest metropolitan areas, where one consultant even offers a $10,000 "concierge" package for the bride who wants to do nothing more than verbally approve the consultant's selections and write checks to pay the suppliers.

To arrive at a price for your wedding packages, Gerard J. Monaghan of the Association of Bridal Consultants suggests using this formula to come up with an hourly rate:

(amount you want to net annually) ÷ 50 weeks
÷ 5 days per week x 2.5 (factor for
expenses) = per diem ÷ 8 hours =
hourly rate

The Small Business Administration says the average for service industry pay rates is $25 to $125 per hour. Where you price your services in this range depends on what your local market will bear. In the next chapter, we'll discuss how to go about researching your market.

Stat Fact
Coordinating ten weddings a year is a good goal to shoot for during the first year of operation, says Gerard J. Monaghan of the Association of Bridal Consultants. An experienced consultant who doesn't have employees can handle about 30 to 40 nuptials per year.

Developing Your
Market

The place to start when establishing your wedding consulting business is with market research. Market research will help you lay the groundwork for creating a viable and successful business. It will help you to identify exactly who might be interested in using your services, and whether the area where you want to set up shop can actually sustain your

Wedding News

Wondering what the world's number-one wedding city is? Forget Paris, the City of Lights, or romantic Venice. The number-one wedding city is Istanbul, Turkey, with almost 170,000 weddings per year.

bridal business. Market research will also provide you with useful information and data that can help you avoid problems down the road.

Now, you might be thinking, "Whoa, there! I'm an aspiring wedding planner, not a statistician. Besides, people get married everywhere. There's bound to be enough business in my area to keep me busy."

Maybe, maybe not. The wedding industry may generate annual retail sales of more than $120 billion, but not every part of the country has the same need for consultants. Take, for instance, those parts of Florida that are heavily populated by senior citizens. It's a safe bet that the chances of making a go at running a successful wedding consultant business in those areas are probably slim to none. Likewise, in rough-and-tumble states like Alaska or Montana, where new jeans are considered formal wear, there is probably a maximum number of consultants the economy can support. Or, if you live in a rural area, there is simply not the population to grow your wedding consultant business beyond a certain level.

You have to think this way if you want to be successful, and the only way you're going to find out about these kinds of shortcomings—as well as the potential opportunities—is by researching your target market. Fortunately, this is something you can undertake yourself even if you don't have a background in statistics or research, says David L. Williams, Ph.D., an associate professor of marketing research at Wayne State University in Detroit.

"With the exception of questionnaire development, which can be difficult for a beginner to do well, you can pretty much handle all of the research by yourself on a reasonably small budget," Williams says. "The problem is, many small business owners view market research as an optional expense. But it's the only accurate way you have to find out what's important to your customer."

This chapter will show you how to find out who will use your services, learn where they live and work, and determine the kinds of services they'll want you to provide. Armed with this information, you'll be able to make informed decisions that can help your business grow and prosper.

Defining Your Audience

As the song says, "Love makes the world go 'round," which means there should be plenty of people who will need your services, right? In theory, yes. But you'll be much more successful if you study the demographics of the area you wish to do business in, then tailor your services to a specific group within that market.

Demographics are defined as the characteristics of the people in your target audience that make them more likely to use your services or products. These characteristics may include age, education, and income level, gender, type of residence, and geographic location.

Stat Fact

In 1999, according to *Modern Bride* magazine, 50 percent of couples used a wedding consultant; by 2002 that number had grown to 62 percent. Industry experts expect this uptick to continue.

Probably the most significant demographic for wedding consultants to consider is age. According to The Knot, an online source of wedding information, the average age of today's bride is 26, while the average age of the groom is 28. So while you certainly can serve people of any age group, you'll probably have the best success and garner the most business if you target brides in their mid-20s. This also means that if the population base in the area where you wish to do business doesn't have brides in this age group, you must either reconsider your market or adjust your marketing strategy.

Case in point: Brides may be the ultimate consumer for your services, but who sometimes foots the bills for those dream weddings? Mom and Dad, of course. As we've already discussed, as men and women are choosing to marry later, many have established careers and opt to pay for their big day. Still, in more rural areas, parents are often the primary payers of wedding day bills.

So, a viable way to adjust your strategy if you aren't based where 20-something consumers live is to target their parents instead. That's what Julia K. of suburban Dallas did when her market research showed that the communities around her were populated by couples who were long-time residents and were likely to have children of marriageable age. As a result, she concentrates her advertising efforts in those communities and now coordinates an average of 30 weddings per year.

This is not to say there's no market for your services among older brides. According to the Stepfamily Association of America, 43 percent of all marriages are remarriages for at least one of the adults. These brides are usually older (early 30s and up) and also are prime candidates for your services given the demands of their careers—and their children.

Yet another factor to consider is where your prospective clients live versus where they work. Julia says that brides may look for information, use bridal registries, or purchase their invitations in the area where they work, but they'll go home to get married. That means the wedding consultant may have to travel if he or she wishes to serve the brides who work in the local business community.

Targeting Professional Women

One demographic segment, which many wedding consultants serve successfully, is that of professional women. These corporate executives or business owners often hold advanced college degrees and have high incomes. Because they don't have time to plan their own weddings, they're more likely to favor full-service packages that make it possible for them to turn all the details over to an experienced planner. Since full-service packages are usually a consultant's highest priced offering, this can translate into significant profits.

Lisa K., the Connecticut-based wedding consultant, makes professional contacts through her membership in a local Chamber of Commerce. "This is just a great way to network and grow my business. So much of this business is word-of-mouth and this is a wonderful way to spread the word."

Stat Fact
Fifty-three percent of recent brides, who did not use wedding consultants, said that planning their weddings interfered with their jobs.

Marsha F. and Jenny C., wedding consultants based in Dallas, found their niche by targeting professional women. Originally, they intended to coordinate high profile and celebrity weddings, but found the market was very difficult to break into. By refocusing their efforts on serving professional women instead, the weddings they book now average $30,000.

Packy B., the wedding consultant in Broadview Heights, Ohio, has also successfully captured the professional woman's market. She often communicates with her executive-level brides solely by e-mail, and has coordinated every detail of some of her most elaborate and lavish weddings this way.

Economic Environment

Before we move on, there's one more very important factor to consider in your market research efforts. That's the economic base in your prospective market area.

Obviously, a wedding consultant is not an absolute necessity when it comes to coordinating a wedding. People get married all the time without ever using consultants' services. What you offer is experience, convenience, and the ability to step in when the details become too time-consuming or overwhelming for a busy bride to manage. So your task not only becomes making your services irresistible to brides, but making sure the people who will pay the bills are financially able to afford your services. This last point is critical because brides and grooms typically go over their initial budget estimates.

Destination Romance

Richard Markel, of the Association for Wedding Professionals International, estimates that at least 12 percent of weddings are destination weddings. The reason? "The internet," he says. "It's given us the capability to find anything anywhere. People are now forming tour companies all around the country just to handle destination events like weddings."

The internet has opened legions of new opportunities for wedding consultants who live and work in highly desirable locations such as Orlando (with Disney World), Hawaii (with its slice of paradise), and New York City (with its cosmopolitan flair). Australia, Europe, and Mexico are also becoming increasingly popular destination wedding sites.

Wedding consultants who are willing to handle the extra challenges involved in coordinating destination weddings may find they're not as restricted by the vagaries of the local economy.

For more information about planning destination weddings and to find out if this type of work meshes with your wedding consultant business plans, check out these books: *The Destination Wedding Workbook* by Paris Permenter and John Bigley (booklocker.com, 2004) or *Destination Bride* by Lisa Light, (F&W Publications, 2005).

"At least half of brides and grooms go over their budgets," says Ann Nola, director of the Association of Certified Professional Wedding Consultants. So, your job is to help manage the budget as well as be straightforward in your billing and payment expectations. If for instance, you decide to take a 10 percent fee of the entire wedding cost and the costs escalate, then you may have a frustrated wedding couple, unable or unwilling to pay their bills. For instance, if the couple plans to spend $25,000 and your contract stipulates that you will take a 10 percent commission, your pay day will net you $2,500. However, if the total wedding costs soar to $35,000, the couple will now, per your contract, owe you $3,500. The bride and groom may be frustrated that you didn't help them tamp down costs, and they may simply not have the money to pay you. So, beware, as you solicit business that the brides- and grooms-to-be will be able to pay for your services.

If you've done your market research right, you already have some idea of the average income levels in your neighborhood. Now you need to look at data like the percentage of people who are employed full-time and the types of jobs they hold. If the local market is driven by blue-collar, heavy, industry jobs, a downturn in the economy could make cash tight and affect your ability to book weddings. So could a plant

▲

shutdown or a scaling back of services. A call to your city's economic development office is an easy way to get a handle on the health of local industry in your area.

While you're at it, ask about the area's white-collar jobs and the types of companies that support them. One industry to be wary of is the high-tech industry. Jobs in the computer and dotcom sectors are red hot right now, as are jobs in the financial field with record bonuses for those in the field. But you only have to glance at the Dow Jones industrial averages to

⚠ **Beware!**
Mailing lists are purchased for one time use. Lists are "seeded" with control names so the seller will know if you use the list more than one time. If you wish to use the list more than once, you'll have to ante up again.

know that tech stocks experience huge swings in both directions. So again, an economy that's based on high-tech jobs has the potential to go south, taking your prospective customers with it. You need to make sure you have a backup survival plan if you aspire to serve an area that's heavily dependent on a single industry.

Conducting Market Research

Now that you have a general idea about the types of people who might be responsive to your marketing efforts, you can proceed to the next step, which is to conduct an organized market research study. Your goal is to touch base with potential customers to find out whether they'd be interested in using the services of a wedding consultant, as well as exactly what types of services they may require.

There are two kinds of research: primary, which is information gathered firsthand; and secondary, which is information culled from external sources. Each has its own merits as well as costs.

Primary Research

The most common forms of primary research used by wedding consultants are direct mail surveys, telemarketing campaigns, and personal interviews. Assuming that you'll want to save your start-up capital for equipment and advertising, you should probably try a survey first since it's the most cost-effective way to gather information. By the same token, you might try doing the survey yourself rather than hiring a marketing research firm because that can be quite expensive.

Your survey should be no more than a page long, since it's difficult to get busy people to fill out anything lengthier. The questions should be well-phrased so they're direct, clear, and unambiguous. They should also be constructed so the information

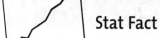

Stat Fact

According to Richard Markel of the Association for Wedding Professionals International, at any given time, just 1 percent of the population is planning a wedding. The trick is to find that part of the 1 percent in your geographic area and target your marketing efforts toward them.

they gather is conducive to analysis. For example, a question like "Would you be interested in hiring a wedding consultant?" isn't very useful because it's closed-ended, meaning it's possible for the respondent to give a "yes" or "no" answer without elaborating. That's not going to give you much insight, which is the whole point of this exercise.

Although you can certainly draft the questions yourself, you should consider asking someone experienced in market research for help. Since a marketing research firm tends to be pricey, Williams, associate professor at Wayne State University, suggests contacting the business school at your local university instead. A marketing professor on staff might be willing to draft your questionnaire for $500 to $1,000, or may even assign your questionnaire as a class project, as Williams himself has done. In the meantime, you'll find a sample market research questionnaire on pages 24–25 that you can use as a guideline.

Surveying the Market

This part is easier than you might think. Start by purchasing a mailing list that's targeted to the market you wish to reach. Local trade associations, list brokers, and even daily newspapers in major metropolitan areas can sell you a list of heads of households that can be sorted in many ways, including by zip code, so you can target a specific geographic area. You can find a huge listing of publications that sell their lists in the Standard Rate and Data Service (VNU) directory, which can be found in many libraries or look online at www.srds.com. Some other criteria you are bound to be interested in will include occupation (if you are looking for professional women), gender (since women are the primary consumers of bridal consulting services), and age (as in 20-ish or the parental age brackets). Need another list source? Try the Directory of Associations (Gale Research), which can be found at most large libraries or at www.marketingsource.com.

Smart Tip

Tip...

Don't stint on your market research. Studies show that doing thorough market research convinces your clients that you care about their needs and that you will listen carefully to their concerns. Also, it takes the guesswork out of your service and developing business plans.

Market Research Questionnaire

Special Occasions Bridal Consulting

1010 Park Avenue
Lincoln Park, Michigan 10101

June 13, 200x

Ms. Susan Pfeiffer
10 Spring Lake Road
Bloomfield Hills, Michigan 10101

Dear Ms. Pfeiffer:

Congratulations on your recent engagement! This is an exciting time in your life, and I wish you much happiness.

I am about to start a wedding consulting business in the metro Detroit area that will assist happy brides-to-be like you with the many details necessary to organize a picture-perfect wedding. Would you please take a few minutes to answer the following questions so I can assist brides like you better?

What is your age?

❑ 18–24   ❑ 35–39

❑ 25–29   ❑ 40–44

❑ 30–34   ❑ 45 and up

Which of the following services might interest you as you plan your wedding? (Check all that apply.)

❑ Assistance with setting up and staying within budget

❑ Information about reliable vendors (i.e., florists, caterers, bakers, etc.)

❑ Assistance with selecting and meeting with vendors

❑ Assistance with planning your entire wedding

Market Research Questionnaire, continued

❑ Services of a wedding consultant on the wedding day

❑ Services of a wedding consultant to handle the entire event

❑ Coordination of the rehearsal dinner

❑ Handling of honeymoon arrangements

Have you ever considered using a wedding consultant?

❑ Yes   ❑ No

Would you prefer to pay a flat fee or a percentage of your wedding costs for wedding consultant services?

❑ Flat fee   ❑ Percentage

If you hired a consultant who charged a flat fee, how much would you be willing to pay?

❑ $1,000–$1,500

❑ $1,501–$2,000

❑ $2,001–$2,500

❑ more than $2,500, depending on the complexity of the wedding

What is your household income?

❑ $25,000–$50,000   ❑ $50,001–$75,000   ❑ $75,000 and up

What is your educational level?

❑ High school diploma   ❑ College degree

❑ Graduate school degree   ❑ Doctorate degree

What is your profession?

_____

_____

If you would like to be contacted by a wedding consultant, provide your phone number here:

( ) _____

Beware!

Most wedding consultants agree that attendees at bridal shows are a tougher sell. Brides-to-be often attend bridal shows precisely because they feel they can't afford a wedding consultant. These brides-to-be have decided that meeting vendors at the bridal show will serve in lieu of hiring a consultant. If you decide to buy a list of those attending a bridal show, make sure the cost for the list fits into your business budget and have realistic expectations regarding the number of surveys you expect to be completed and returned. If you do decide to send your questionnaire to bridal show attendees, you may be able to purchase a copy of the list directly from the trade show organizer.

Once you have your list in hand (which is usually priced as a flat rate per 1,000 names), you're ready to produce your questionnaire. To keep the cost down, format it yourself on a home computer, then bop over to a quick print shop like Kinko's or Staples and have copies run off on your company letterhead.

Cash as Bait

How would you like an easy way to improve your response rates? Try enclosing a crisp, new dollar bill with your survey. The dollar is sent as a thank you to the recipient for taking the time to fill out and return the questionnaire. Although it does not guarantee a response, the buck certainly is an attention-getter, and direct marketing studies have shown that sending even a small cash honorarium does tend to improve the rate of return.

Of course, this trick could cost you a pretty penny, so to speak, since Williams says that surveys should be sent to a sample of at least 300 people to get useful data. However, even as few as 100 surveys would be useful, and would only require a $100 investment if you choose to include a monetary incentive.

Pick Up the Phone

Since you probably love people and already have strong people skills if you're planning to get into a service industry like wedding consulting, telemarketing is a natural, if time-consuming, way to gather information. As with surveys, you'll need a strong telemarketing script with questions similar to those on your market research questionnaire and a good prospect list. But when you call, don't just fill out the form. Listen carefully to the person on the other end of the line. She's bound to make comments and have concerns about things you've never even considered. That helps you add to the storehouse of knowledge you'll tap into when you're ready to go after your first client.

A Job for the Pros

If you're really nervous about doing your own market research and have a sufficiently large start-up budget, you could engage a market research firm to help you. These firms are located in most large cities and will be listed in the Yellow Pages. They will not only collect information for you; they'll also handle all incoming data, then analyze the results, and prepare a report for your review.

Williams says a smaller firm might charge you $2,000 to $3,000 to handle a survey project and prepare a simple report. The cost for 200 to 300 interviews and a report would be about $4,000 to $8,000.

Secondary Research

If you're looking for real cost savings when doing market research, try using secondary research. Someone, somewhere has probably researched something that relates to what you want to know, and you can often put your hands on that information free of charge.

The mother lode of statistical information can be found at state and federal agencies, since they collect data on everything from income levels to buying habits. Although this data may be a year or two old, it can still be very useful, particularly for the fledgling wedding consultant who does not have much money to spend on research. Some great sources of information are the U.S. Census Bureau (www.census.gov), the Small Business Development Administration (www.sba.gov), local economic development organizations, and even utility companies, which often have demographic data they will provide free of charge or for a very nominal fee.

Other sources of useful secondary research include your local library and chamber of commerce, your state's economic development department, trade associations, and trade publications. You can find the names of thousands of trade publications in Standard Rate and Data Service (VNU). And of course, the internet is an invaluable source of just about any information you require. Just be sure to gather information only from reputable sites, such as those posted by organizations with good business reputations or those that appear to have rock solid data sources themselves.

Finally, simply be aware of the news that is available to you every day. Read your local newspaper. This is an invaluable resource. Is the local manufacturing plant closing? Your local paper will give you the most up-to-date news. If you live in a less populous area and the plant closing results in large lay-offs, this will affect your business plans. Local papers also track trends—perhaps you live in an area that is rapidly expanding. Your local paper will report on this. Put another way, keep your ears and eyes open to the

Tip...

Smart Tip

Consider doing your information gathering via the Internet. This can often prove to be a relatively inexpensive and time-efficient way of gathering important data. Check out *Email Marketing: Using Email to Reach Your Target Audience and Build Customer Relationships* by Jim Sterne and Anthony Priore (Wiley, 2000). This comprehensive guide shows how to ace this cheap and easy-to-use tool, including do's and don'ts and real-world examples.

world around you, and you will find that this information is invaluable to your developing business.

Writing a Mission Statement

Understanding your market and the people you'll serve is critical to the success of your business. But understanding yourself and defining exactly what you plan to do as a wedding consultant is equally important. So follow the lead of America's most successful corporations and write a simple mission statement that includes your company's goals and outlines how you will fulfill them.

What might a typical mission statement for a wedding consulting business say? Here are a couple of examples:

Bride's Choice will serve the needs of busy professional women by providing a full range of wedding consultation services. Thanks to my prior hands-on experience with wedding planning for several friends and family members, I am confident that I will be able to coordinate ten weddings in my first year of operation.

Here's another possible approach to a mission statement:

Hearts and Flowers Inc. is poised to become the premier wedding consultant service in greater Ashtabula. With our network of reliable suppliers, our personal background in business management, and our extensive network of social and business contacts, we bring an extra measure of experience to the business that will inspire confidence in our clients. Our goal is to achieve sales of $50,000 in calendar year 2007.

Your mission statement is your compass as well as the foundation on which your business' future is built. It can be one sentence long, as in the case of Pepsi's mission statement—whose succinct version is "Beat Coke"—or it can be several paragraphs. The length doesn't matter; the direction it provides is what's important. We've provided a worksheet on page 30 to get you thinking about what you want to include in the mission statement for your business.

Importance of a Mission

Don't underestimate the importance of a mission statement. It absolutely affects the direction of your growing business. Take time to clearly elucidate your thoughts and then follow these guidelines suggested by www.bplans.com:

○ Tell who your company is, what you do, what you stand for, and why you do it.

○ Never use more than three or four sentences. Many experts suggest using only one pithy sentence.

○ If you can't remember your mission statement, then no one else will either.

○ No hyperbole!

○ Look at other mission statements.

○ Believe in your mission statement.

Consider Avon's mission statement:

To be the company that best understands and satisfies the product, service, and self-fulfillment needs of women globally.

This is a powerful and comprehensive statement—and all wrapped up in one elegant sentence.

Mission Statement Worksheet

Here's your opportunity to try your hand at writing your own mission statement. Start out by answering the following questions:

1. What are your reasons for becoming a wedding consultant?

   _____

   _____

2. What are your personal objectives? How do you intend to achieve them?

   _____

   _____

3. What skills do you bring to the business that will be of benefit?

   _____

   _____

4. What is your vision for this business? Where do you think you can take it in one, two, and five years?

   _____

   _____

   _____

Using this information, write your mission statement here:

Mission Statement for

_____

(your company name)

_____

_____

_____

_____

_____

Building the Foundations of Your Business

Just as a bridal gown has a couture "superstruc-ture" made of satin overlays, lace insets, and rustling tulle, a wedding consulting business needs a formal framework to ensure compliance with commonly accepted business prac-tices. This chapter delves into standard operating procedures for everything from legal matters to business insurance and

shows you how to get your business machine oiled, cranked up, and ready to run.

It's All in a Name

Just as developing a mission statement was critical in the development of your business plan and strategy, so too is choosing a name for your company. Making this selection should be high on your list of priorities in the early stages of business development.

We've all heard the axiom that "it's all in a name." Take this to heart because your name may very well help to set your potential client's opinion of you and the services you offer.

Many wedding consultants opt to use their own names combined with a business description, like "Eileen Figure Bridal Consulting." But this can present a problem when it comes to cashing checks. If a client makes out a check to the business name rather than to you, your bank probably isn't going to cash it. Then you'll have to ask the client to issue another check, which can make you seem unprofessional. In addition, using this type of name can lead to confusion with the IRS because it may be harder for those busy bureaucrats to distinguish between your personal income and your business income.

Even so, it is possible to incorporate your own name in the business name if that's what you really want. One wedding consultant in Austin, Texas, did this successfully when she named her home based business "Elegant Weddings by Donna."

Robbi Ernst, President of June Wedding, Inc., strongly advises against using your name when naming your new business.

"One should not use a personal name, i.e., "Weddings by Dorothy" or "Lara's Weddings." The rationale for this is that someday they may want to retire or otherwise want to get out of the business and do something else, and they will want to be able to sell the company. The very real problem with using a personal name for the company is that unless the person who buys the company is named Dorothy or Lara, they will have to change the name. Through the years of its life, a company builds a reputation for integrity, quality, professionalism, and creativity. That reputation has a monetary value and is part of what a buyer is purchasing."

Generally speaking, you should select a catchy, creative name that identifies who you are without being too cute. That means staying away from names that are over-the-top, like "Smart Broads Wedding Service," "Hugs and Kisses Weddings," or "Your First Wedding." Not only are they not professional, they won't inspire confidence in your clientele.

Simple, business-like names are always a better choice. Another of the wedding consultants interviewed for this book chose her romantic-sounding name, "Ever After Weddings," specifically because she didn't want her own name in the title.

"It seems to me that these are not ever my weddings and by using a name like 'Weddings by Lisa,' it implies control," she says. "That's a myth [about wedding consulting] that I wanted to discredit, not encourage."

Deborah McCoy, of the American Academy of Wedding Professionals, instructs that, "wedding consultants must ask themselves: What makes me different? What makes me unique? Am I going to specialize in upscale affairs or a wide range of parties?"

There can be other compelling reasons for a name choice. Dolores E., the wedding consultant in Larkspur, California, started her business in 1991 under one name. In 1999 she took a well-deserved sabbatical, then decided to reopen the business

---

Everyone Can Have a June Wedding

When you create a name for your business, remember that you are not only selling a product but also a vision of a perfect wedding day, a day on which dreams will come true. It's a big responsibility, selecting a name that's clever and evocative, yet accurately describes what you do.

Robbi Ernst, President of June Wedding Inc., describes how he arrived at the name for his successful consulting business. "I had a lot of fun selecting the name for my company. In coming up with the name of "June Wedding," we purposefully chose the month of June since this is popular jargon in wedding industry talk; but, in particular, it was purely a marketing tool that we chose the singular June Wedding as opposed to the plural June Weddings. This was with the idea that everyone can have a June Wedding, even if they get married in the cold of a snowy winter, or the sweltering and humid heat of August. We added the Inc., when we formed the company into a corporation."

under a new name that started with the letter "A." The reason? "I'm now first in the phone book," Dolores says.

Nancy Tucker of Coordinators' Corner agrees. "Consider how the name you are choosing explains the job you do. Also, consider the alpha placing of the name wherever it will be listed."

Not everyone can be listed in that coveted first spot, but you can choose a unique name that's distinctive and evocative of what your business does. To help you get started, check the Yellow Pages for ideas (as well as to avoid duplication). Or you can do what Loreen C., the wedding consultant in Ypsilanti, Michigan, did before settling on a business name. After polling her friends, she came up with a list of about 50 names, which she narrowed down to ten finalists. Then she put those names to a vote before deciding on her highly descriptive name. She knew she made the right choice when she was in the post office one day and a woman who saw her carrying a box with her return address asked if she planned weddings.

"You need a name that catches the eye and provides instant recognition of what you do," Loreen stresses. "That day in the post office proved my business name did both."

We have included a worksheet on page 35 to help you select an appropriate moniker. Once you have picked a suitable name, it's time to move on to the next step: setting up your business structure.

When you have selected a name make sure that someone else hasn't already laid claim to it. You can do your own name search for free if you have access to the internet. Check for trademarks registered nationally on the U.S. Patent and Trademark Office web site at www.uspto.gov. You can also search for the name using popular portals like America Online, Yahoo!, Google, and Lycos. Network Solutions (www.networksolutions.com) can tell you if there's a web site that already uses the name you've chosen.

Smart Tip

If you plan on keeping your business small, there is no need to trademark your name. However, if you have plans to grow your company or have come up with an original and especially catchy name, you may want to consider federal trademark protection. The Federal Trademark Registration is done through the Library of Congress in Washington, DC.

Registering Your Company Name

Most states require you to register your fictitious company name officially to ensure that it's unique. This is usually done at the county level, and is known as filing a DBA ("doing business as") statement. The fee to file is usually

Name that Business

Establishing a unique business identity is not just important; it's absolutely essential so prospective clients (and, alas, the IRS) can find you easily. Try the following brainstorming exercise to whittle down your choices and find the perfect name.

List the top three things that come to mind when you hear the word "wedding" (such as bride or bouquet). Be creative!

1. _____
2. _____
3. _____

List three unique landmarks or features that characterize the place where you'll do business (such as the sand dunes of northern Michigan or the picturesque caves of Carlsbad).

1. _____
2. _____
3. _____

List three geographical references (such as your city, state, or regional area).

1. _____
2. _____
3. _____

Now, try combining elements from these three sections in different ways:

1. _____
2. _____
3. _____

Did you come up with something you liked? If not, try using alliteration ("Weddings in White") or plays on words ("Altared State") with any of the elements above to create a business name.

Once you've selected a name, put it to the test:

O Say it aloud several times to make sure it's easily understood, both in person and over the phone. A name like "Simply Sensational Celebrations" has too many "s" sounds and may be difficult to pronounce, let alone understand on the phone.

O Page through your local Yellow Pages directory to make sure someone else isn't already using the name you've chosen.

O Check with your county seat or other official registrar to make sure the name is available. Someone may have already claimed the name but may not be using it yet.

O Does your name pass the test? Way to go! Now you're ready to register it officially.

nominal (around $30 to $60) and entitles you to use the name for a limited period of time, usually three years. When the time expires, you simply renew the DBA. Before you get your DBA, however, a search is done to make sure your name is unique. If you happen to choose a name that's already being used, you'll have to pick something else, so it's a good idea to have a couple of names in reserve.

Your Corporate Structure

Once you have your DBA in hand, you are considered the proud owner of a legitimate business. So naturally, the IRS will have something to say about the way you run it. (You knew we'd get around to the IRS eventually, didn't you?) Basically, this means the bureaucrats in Washington require that you operate as one of four business entities: a sole proprietorship, a corporation, a partnership, or a limited liability company (LLC).

Sole Proprietors

Most wedding consultants choose to operate as sole proprietors because it's the easiest type of business to form. All you have to do is file a DBA as discussed above, then open a business checking account in that name. You can use your personal credit card to pay for business expenditures, yet you still get tax benefits like business expense deductions. But there is a downside to the sole proprietorship. You are personally liable for any losses, bankruptcy claims, legal actions, and so on. That can wipe out both your personal and business assets if a catastrophe hits.

General Partnership

If you are planning to join forces with another wedding consultant to open a business, you are forming a general partnership. Partnerships are easier to form than corporations, and you don't have to file any documents to make them legal. But since each partner is responsible for the actions of the other, it's a good idea to have a partnership agreement drawn up by an attorney. That way, you can spell out exactly what each person is responsible for.

Limited Liability Company

A third type of business entity is the limited liability company, or LLC, which combines the tax structure of a partnership, yet protects the business owner from personal liability. This is the type of partnership agreement Marsha B. and Jenny C., the wedding consultants in Dallas, drew up when they started their business. Even though they had known each other for 25 years and brought complementary skills to the partnership that have made it flourish, they recognized how important it was to protect their personal interests.

"I have a sole proprietorship now, but I'm thinking about establishing an LLC in a year or two," says Loreen C., the wedding consultant in Michigan. "I'm still researching the benefits, but I think it's important to have protection so no one can touch my personal property. I wouldn't want anything taken away from my family."

Corporations

The last type of business arrangement is the corporation. It is established as a totally separate legal entity from the business owner. Establishing a corporation requires filing articles of incorporation, electing officers, and holding an annual meeting. Not many wedding consultants choose this route initially because the costs are prohibitive, and the company must pay corporate taxes. On the other hand, a corporation will find it easier to obtain financing, which would be useful if you decided to franchise your business, start a retail store that caters to brides, or expand in a big way.

Robbi Ernst of June Wedding, Inc., recommends incorporation. "I constantly urge new business owners to file as a corporation. Corporation status is especially important if you have a lot of assets or if one has a family."

Incidentally, if you operate under your own name, you can use your social security number when filing your business taxes. But if you adopt another name for your sole proprietorship, or form a partnership or corporation, you are required to have a federal employment identification number (EIN). To apply for one, pick up a copy of form SS-4 at any IRS office, or print one off the web site at www.irs.ustreas.gov. If you are not sure which business arrangement to choose, talk to an attorney experienced in handling small business issues.

"There are advantages to each kind of entity, and an attorney can help you decide which one is best for your situation," says Daniel H. Minkus, chairman of the business law section of the State Bar of Michigan, and a member of the business practice group of Clark Hill PLC. "If you don't know the people you are doing business with, I'd encourage you to form a single-member LLC or corporation. They're simple to create, and they're invaluable because your clients are dealing with your enterprise and not you personally."

If you choose to incorporate without using an attorney, it will cost you $150 to $450 to do it yourself, versus $500 to $1,000 if you choose to have an attorney handle the process. Corporate law is complex and difficult to understand, so it is often advisable to allow a professional to handle this for you. You'll find information about hiring an attorney in Chapter 5.

Beware!
Zoning regulations are established at the local (city, township, or village) level rather than the state level. A homebased business that's perfectly legal in one city could be verboten in another. The only way to find out is by calling the zoning board in your community.

Choosing a Business Site

Just when you thought it was safe to test the waters with your new business, you find out there could be a restriction on your activities. That could come in the form of a local zoning ordinance, which prohibits businesses to operate in certain areas like residential neighborhoods. Such ordinances exist to protect people from excessive traffic and noise (as well as to rake in the extra taxes assessed on businesses). But because your business doesn't require signage, and you won't have a lot of people coming and going, it's quite likely you can run the business quietly from your home. Still, to be on the safe side, you should check with your local government office to see if any special permits are required. It's better to find out upfront, before you go to the expense of printing stationery and obtaining a business telephone line, than to find out later that homebased businesses are prohibited in your area.

It's especially important to check local zoning regulations if you plan to do consultations with prospective clients in your home. You may need to establish a business office elsewhere, as Julia K., the wedding consultant in Oak Point, Texas, did when she rented a 1,500 square foot townhouse and converted it into a business office separate from her home.

Other Licenses and Permits

But wait, there's more! Some municipalities require business owners to have a business license. It's usually available for a very nominal fee and is renewable annually. If by chance you are turned down for a license because of zoning restrictions, you can apply for (and probably receive) a variance from the municipal planning commission so you can get your license.

Then there's the health department permit that's necessary from the county where you do business, if you provide any of the food at your weddings. A permit is also necessary if you bake the wedding cake yourself, says Donna H. An experienced baker who started out in the wedding industry by baking cakes for military personnel on a local base, Donna doesn't trust the job to anyone else. So she dutifully pays for her health certificate every year so she can continue her personal tradition of baking for her brides.

To find out whether you need other special permits or licenses, you can contact:

- *Small Business Administration (SBA)*. See the federal listings in your phone book, or go to www.sba.gov.
- *Small Business Development Center (SBDC)*. Reachable through the SBA, or by logging onto www.sba.gov.
- *Service Corps of Retired Executives (SCORE)*. Go to www.score.org. This non-profit organization is an SBA partner and has hundreds of chapters throughout the United States.

Writing a Business Plan

There's still one more task you have to complete before you can leave this chapter and plunge into the other uncharted waters that await you. And this is a big one—one that literally can make or break your business.

You have to write a scintillating, compelling, and painfully comprehensive business plan that will guide you though the aforementioned Bermuda Triangle of Business.

Your business plan is like a roadmap. It outlines your plans, goals, and strategies for making your business successful. It's useful not just for applying for credit or attracting investors. It also gives you direction so you can achieve even your loftiest goals as well as measure the success of your business over time.

Experts say that a thoroughly researched business plan is about 25 pages long and takes 300 hours to prepare (which includes doing research, compiling financial information, conducting surveys, and writing). This may seem like a drag, but a plan that's too sketchy will neither keep you on the right course, nor help you find the financing you may need.

There are seven major components a business plan should have. Here's how they apply to a bridal consulting business:

1. *Executive summary*. In this section, which summarizes the entire business plan, describe the nature of your business, the scope of the services you offer (including brief details about the various wedding packages you'll offer, additional services like retail goods sales and so on), the legal form of operation (discussed earlier

Tip...

Smart Tip

Plan on writing your business plan yourself. This plan should reflect your voice and your identity, not that of a professional writer. Don't focus on flash, rather focus on content, the concrete goals of your developing business. If you don't trust your grammar and editing skills, hire an editor to check over the finished product—to check for errors, *not* to change the tone and style.

in this chapter), and your goals. If you plan to use the business plan to seek financing for your company, you should include details about your future plans for the business, too.

Smart Tip

The Small Business Association is a wonderful resource for easy-to-follow and comprehensive information to guide you through the development and writing of your business plan. Check their web site for more information at www.sba.gov.

2. *Business description.* In this section, you'll want to describe both the bridal industry and your target market. You'll find general statistics about the bridal industry in the guide you're holding. But for even more information that can prove helpful in establishing the viability of your business, check the Small Business Development Center web site at www.sba.gov/gopher/local-information/small-business-development-centers.

3. *Market strategies.* Here's another place where all that market research data will come in handy. In this section, you'll want to analyze exactly what you'll do to reach prospective brides and how you'll pull it off. Focus, too, on the things that make your company unique, from your personal experience in event planning, to specialized business know-how or other factors. You'll find more information about marketing plans in Chapter 3.

4. *Competitive analysis.* If you have done your homework well, you already know how many wedding consultants are in business in your target market area. But in this section, you should also consider other potential competitors, such as general event planners who also coordinate weddings and banquet facilities that offer consulting services. Analyze their strengths and weaknesses, and contrast them against what you perceive to be your own strengths. Also, don't forget to consider the aspects that make your services unique and special.

5. *Design and development plan.* Here's where you will consider how you will develop market opportunities to help your company prosper and grow. It's helpful to create a timetable of objectives that you can refer to as benchmarks for your successes, like setting a goal for graduating from ten weddings a year to 20 and how much contract help you'll need to accomplish this.

6. *Operations and management plan.* You can use the information in Chapter 2 of this manual, which discusses the day-to-day operations of your business, as a guide for drafting this section. You should keep this section of your marketing plan updated to reflect any new or expanded services you offer.

7. *Financial factors.* Even if you're a sole proprietor with very modest first-year expectations, you need to forecast the success of your business. This will help keep your business on track and help you avoid nasty surprises later on.

Probably the most important document in this section is your balance sheet, which will provide a running tally of how well your business is doing.

Constructing such a detailed business plan may sound like a lot of nonessential work, especially since you're probably operating out of your den or from your dining room table. But embarking on a new business without a clear-cut plan is like sailing for Europe without a navigational chart or a compass. Without a plan, you won't have any idea to whom you're selling your services or what they're even interested in. So take the time to formalize your business plan now, then refer back to it periodically for both inspiration and direction.

5

Professional
Guidance

Just as a busy bride will turn over the details of planning her wedding extravaganza to you, so you will want to relinquish some of the details of running your business to other professionals who have the expertise to do the job right. Even if you have the know-how to do your own taxes or review

Wedding News

According to Hallmark, 48 percent of wedding cards are sold during the summer months, May through August.

a real estate lease, this isn't necessarily a good use of your time. It's almost always better to spend the lion's share of your working hours on the activity you do best—wedding planning—and rely on other professionals to keep your business humming along behind the scenes. This chapter will give you insight into why you should consider hiring an attorney, an accountant, and an insurance agent, as well as look at what you can expect them to do for you.

Hiring an Attorney

You're reliable and prompt, conscientious and professional. So you couldn't possibly ever have to worry about being sued by one of your sweet, blushing brides or the members of her family, right?

Wrong. Unfortunately, whenever a job involves working with the public, the potential to be sued exists. The lawsuit could be over a matter that you couldn't possibly have controlled, like a sudden torrential downpour that flooded the streets and trapped the caterer in her car on a low-lying street, so the mostaccioli didn't arrive until after the guests did. Or it could be over something more unthinkable, such as having one of your contract workers show up tipsy and unruly, and fall face-first into the cake.

So it makes sense to retain an attorney before anything ever goes wrong so you have someone to turn to for advice and guidance when the time comes. The main reasons a wedding consultant might have for hiring an attorney include:

- Wanting to form a partnership or a corporation
- Finding the language in a contract difficult to understand
- Signing a contract for a large sum of money or one that will cover a long period of time (such as a long-term lease on an office site)
- Being sued or having someone threatening to sue
- Needing help with tax planning, loan negotiations, or employee contracts

"But above all, protecting yourself from liability is one of the most important things you must do as a small business owner," says Daniel H. Minkus, chairman of the business law section of the State Bar of Michigan, and a member of the business practice group of Clark Hill PLC. "An attorney can help you assess your risk for being party to a lawsuit and help you minimize it."

As we discussed in the last chapter, establishing an LLC or a corporation is a good way to limit the liability on your personal property. Limiting your financial liability when hiring an attorney is just as important, especially when you're just starting out, and your cash flow is modest. Minkus says that because you don't need a litigator (someone who will defend you in court against lawsuits) to handle your legal work at the outset, you can keep the cost down by hiring an attorney in a one- or two-person practice.

Attorneys' hourly rates typically run from $100 to $450, with the higher rates being charged by senior partners and those who work at larger firms. Other factors that influence cost

Smart Tip Tip...

Turn to the internet for help when hiring an attorney. lawyers.com offers advice on everything from determining when you should seek the sage advice of a lawyer to guiding you through the preparations you'll need to make before meeting with an attorney.

include geographic location, the experience of the attorney, and the attorney's area of expertise.

You may be required to pay an initial consultation fee, so it's important to ask about this before you ever set foot in the lawyer's office. In addition, you may have to pay

Choosing the Right Attorney

When choosing a lawyer, make sure that her personality works well with yours. When interviewing a prospective attorney, consider these questions:

○ What's your background and experience?
○ What's your specialty?
○ How long have you been practicing?
○ Do you have other consultants or small business owners as clients?
○ Have you ever represented a wedding consultant before?
○ Will you do most of the work, or will a paralegal or other aide help out?
○ Is there a charge for an initial consultation?
○ What do you charge for routine legal work?
○ Do you work on a contingency basis?

Also, make sure that the attorney will meet with you in person for this preliminary interview. If she is reluctant to do so, consider a different attorney. For more information, check with your state Bar Association or the American Bar Association. Finally, check the attorney's web site and Yellow Pages ad. Are they tasteful and appealing to you? Often, an attorney's advertisements speak volumes.

your attorney a retainer upfront, which he or she will draw against as work is completed. Others work on a contingency basis, which means they will take a percentage of any lawsuit settlement that's reached. Still others charge a flat fee for routine work, such as filing incorporation papers.

Another way to keep your legal costs reasonable is simply by being organized. "Do your own legwork to gather the information you need beforehand, then limit the number of office visits you must make," Minkus advises. "You also should limit the number of phone calls you make to your attorney, because you'll be charged for those, too."

Many attorneys offer start-up packages that are often more affordable for the small business owner. While you usually can tailor such packages to meet your needs, they typically include an initial consultation, as well as all activities related to the LLC or incorporation process, including the filing of paperwork with your state and other corporate formalities. You can expect to pay approximately $500 if you're establishing an LLC, or $900 if you're setting up a corporation. A payment plan may be available to help you handle the cost.

Locating an attorney you like and respect is often as simple as asking friends or relatives for a referral. In any event, Minkus says that process is much more reliable than just opening the Yellow Pages and picking someone at random. Another way to find a lawyer is through attorney referral services, which are located in many counties throughout the United States. You could also call the American Bar Association at (312) 988-5522 or contact them at www.abanet.org, or go online and check out Find an Attorney at www.findanattorney. com, or consult the Martindale-Hubbell Law Directory at www.martindale.com.

Money Managers

It's usually easier to convince a new business owner that he or she needs an accountant more than other business consultants, like attorneys. Most people are either admirably adept or totally clueless when it comes to budgeting, bookkeeping, and other financial matters. But even those who feel comfortable cranking out their personal taxes annually or investing online may blanche at the thought of creating profit and loss statements and other complex documents. That's usually a pretty reliable sign that you need to "book" the services of a professional accountant.

If you're comfortable doing your own bookkeeping and just need tax help, you could hire an enrolled agent instead of an accountant. In addition to preparing your tax return, enrolled agents can represent you before the IRS. They can be found in the Yellow Pages or through the National Association of Enrolled Agents (www.naea.org).

Bright Idea

A Simplified Employee Pension Plan (SEP) is a must for self-employed individuals. It has a higher contribution limit than a traditional IRA (up to 15 percent of business income, depending on your tax situation), and your funds grow tax-deferred. An accountant or financial planner can help you with the paperwork necessary to set up this important retirement savings tool.

An accountant can help you establish an effective record-keeping system, help you keep expenses in line, and monitor cash flow. He or she can also advise you on tax issues, which is crucial because tax law is very complicated and changes frequently. (The IRS alone issues new tax rulings every two hours of every business day!) Tax issues that might be relevant to a wedding consultant include the amount you can deduct annually for business expenses including travel and entertainment, and office equipment; and the amount of money you can deposit to your simplified employee pension plan (SEP) annually.

Like an attorney, an accountant experienced in handling small business tax issues can also advise you whether you should incorporate your business. In addition to protecting your personal assets, incorporating can cut your tax bill, allow you to put more money into your personal investments, and offer other useful benefits.

There are two types of accountants. Certified public accountants, or CPAs, are college-educated and must pass a rigorous certification examination in the state where they do business in order to put those coveted letters after their names. Public accountants aren't certified and don't have to be licensed by the state. While they may be perfectly capable due to their experience, they usually can't represent you before the IRS like CPAs can, if you're called in for an audit.

There's also a plethora of accounting software on the market that can help you crunch the numbers and manage your business accounting. Intuit QuickBooks is the choice of many small business owners. Keep in mind, however, that some packages may not satisfy IRS requirements for record-keeping. It's probably wiser to rely on a professional to handle accounting matters whenever you need to do anything more complex than record credits and debits, or informally tally up business expenditures.

Smart Tip

Accountants charge anywhere from $75 to $150 an hour and up. Make sure you are not paying them for work you could be doing yourself. For instance, make sure that all of your financial records and receipts are in apple pie order before meeting with your accountant. Being organized will help you to save big money.

To find an accountant, ask your attorney, banker, or other professionals in the wedding industry for a referral. The American Institute of Certified Public Accountants branch in your state can also refer you to a qualified number cruncher, or you can go to their web site at www.aicpa.org. It's very important to select someone who has experience either with small business clients in general, or wedding consultants in particular (although this can be a tall order depending on your area of the country). Avoid accountants who specialize in large corporations, since they're not as likely to be as tuned into your tax and financial situation as you'd like.

Covering Your Assets

The other business professional you should have on your side is an insurance agent. Although you could use one of the services that guide you to discount insurance brokers via the internet, it's probably better to find an agent in your own community instead (or at least at the time of start-up; you can comparison shop and switch later). This will allow you to discuss the particulars of your own business with an agent to make sure you're covered against all potential pitfalls. Face-to-face interaction really is the best way to accomplish this.

Working personally with an agent is also the only reliable way for you to get adequate coverage. An experienced agent will be familiar with the risks you might encounter in your business and can recommend exactly how much coverage you need to protect yourself against those risks.

Locating an insurance agent who can help you with your business needs can be as simple as contacting the person who currently insures your home, apartment, or automobile. However, you should be aware that not all insurance companies (including some of the largest ones) insure homebased businesses. If your insurance provider doesn't offer business insurance, try contacting industry associations for referrals, or simply consult the phone book under "Insurance." Important note: You may find that an independent insurance agent is the best choice for small business insurance. A number of the larger companies we contacted immediately directed us to such agents when we phoned for information.

Insurance Riders

Most insurance companies offer a broad spectrum of insurance plans that can be tailor made for a homebased business owner. In some cases, supplemental insurance policies can be attached to your existing insurance as riders, or addendum to your main policy. Because they "ride" along with the main policy, they don't require the rewriting of your policy.

If you already have standard homeowner's insurance, you may have a certain amount of general liability insurance already built in so you won't need a rider. For

Dollar Stretcher

If you find you need several different types of business insurance, you might want to look for an independent insurance agent or an insurance broker who can shop around for the best rates on each one. Agents who are aligned with just one company will be locked into its rates, which may be higher than what the competition charges. Check your state's insurance department for a list of reputable brokers.

instance, AAA of Michigan includes $2,500 of business equipment replacement insurance in its standard home insurance policy, rather than offering a rider. But if this isn't enough coverage (and it may not be if you have very expensive equipment or will be warehousing retail merchandise in your home), it's usually most affordable to add an insurance rider that offers computer and other business equipment replacement coverage, since most standard homeowner's policies will only cover a fraction of the replacement cost of equipment that's damaged or destroyed. The other type of insurance rider you should consider is one for general liability that protects you and any employees or contractors you hire against business-related personal injury claims.

Riders are generally quite inexpensive; they can be as low as $20 per year for each rider, depending on where you live and do business, and how much insurance you need. Companies that offer riders for homebased businesses include Allstate and Hartford.

Riders generally only protect businesses with less than $5,000 in sales, which is often enough for a wedding consultant who is just starting off in the business. But if your business is more successful, you will need a home business insurance policy instead. This type of insurance provides general liability as well as income loss protection when you can't work. Rates can vary widely depending on where you do business and which company provides the coverage. For example, a general in-home liability policy with State Farm will cost $350 to $475 for $300,000 worth of insurance, $5,000 of which is earmarked specifically as business property insurance. On the other hand, an independent insurance agent we contacted offers a $500,000 general liability policy (with a $5,000 limit for home contents, including computer equipment) for just $150 per year.

Beware!

You may choose to do your own legal and accounting work but absolutely do not consider operating your business without some type of liability insurance. Even if you are very careful and conscientious, you never know when you will find yourself a party in a lawsuit, or the victim of a break-in or an act of God like a tornado or earthquake. A low-cost insurance policy could save your business from bankruptcy in the aftermath of any kind of catastrophic loss, either man-made or natural.

Building a Strong Foundation

Be sure to address these essentials when getting your business started.

❑ Write a mission statement that reflects your company goals accurately and completely.

❑ Select a business name and apply for a DBA.

❑ Consult with an attorney regarding the best legal form for your business.

❑ Apply for an employer identification number (Form SS-4), if you're forming a corporation.

❑ Determine the business location, in-home or at another site.

❑ Check local zoning regulations to determine compliance.

❑ Apply for a business license if required in your community.

❑ Apply for a health department permit if you're planning to serve food or bake wedding cakes.

❑ Write your business plan.

❑ Contact an accountant to discuss the financial and tax requirements related to establishing and operating your business.

❑ Meet with an insurance agent and arrange for adequate insurance.

As one State Farm insurance agent puts it, "It is a very emotional day—and, if the limo is late, the caterer doesn't show up and everything bad happens, even if it's not the consultant's fault, the wedding couple might choose to sue her anyway."

Be safe, be insured.

Business Owner's Insurance

When you start calling around for insurance, you may discover that many general liability policies are available for homebased businesses only if you are running a low traffic business. If you plan to conduct bridal consultations in your home frequently, or if you will hire many independent contractors who will actually work at your home, you are likely to need business owner's insurance instead. This type of insurance provides coverage against physical injuries to your customers and employees, damage to the property of others while on your property (such as damage to a bride's car when it's parked in your driveway), and other situations. This kind of coverage is separate from your homeowner's policy and can cost $350 to $450 per year for $500,000 of coverage from an independent agent, or $150 to $300 for $300,000 from a company like State Farm.

Finally, if you decide to establish your wedding consultant business in a location away from your home, you'll need commercial business insurance. The amount of insurance you will need depends on the type of business you run (and generally speaking, liability for a service business like wedding consultation is low), as well as state or municipal regulations. Your insurance agent can guide you in these matters, but you can also contact your local government to find out what the regulations are.

The Cost of
Doing Business

Anyone who has developed a business—
large or small—will confirm the truth of the axiom that it takes
money to make money.

Fortunately, though, the wedding consultant business is one career opportunity that does not require a large
capital commitment up front. In fact, with careful planning and

Wedding News

According to a survey conducted by the University of Texas, the odds for a long marriage favor those marrying between the ages of 23 and 27.

by shopping carefully for your initial supplies, you may easily be off and running with an investment of as little as $1,000. Of course, this nominal sum assumes that you have some equipment on hand. According to U.S. Census Bureau data, the majority of households in the United States already have a computer. Although we will look at specific requirements later in this chapter—for instance, how much speed and hard drive capabilities your computer should have—you may choose to start your business with a somewhat less up-to-date computer. Yes, computer tasks will take a bit more time, but you won't have to invest as much money upfront in your developing business.

Additionally, because most wedding consultant businesses begin as homebased businesses, start-up costs are relatively low. You don't have the overhead associated with renting an office space. Your dining room table will suffice as a desk, at least initially, and your home telephone can pinch hit as your business line during regular business hours.

This chapter will help you take a systematic approach to estimating your start-up costs so you'll know whether you need to seek outside financing.

Tools of the Trade

The basics you must have to get your business off the ground will include office equipment, including furniture and business machines like computers, and office supplies. You'll find a chart on page 61 with estimates of the equipment start-up costs for two hypothetical businesses. Keep in mind that you may be able to kick off your business by spending even less, by using equipment you already own. It is a good idea to take a thorough inventory of what you already own, from the major items like computers and digital cameras to the smaller items such as paper clips and staplers.

Office Equipment

One of the largest expenditures you'll make at the advent of your new career will be on your

Beware!
As tempting as it may be, don't even think about investing in retail merchandise or props that can be used at weddings until you've been in business for a while. You don't need the extra financial burden when you start out. You don't even have to invest in an extensive business wardrobe as long as you already own attire that would be appropriate for business meetings, bridal consultations, and on-site wedding coordination.

office furniture. Although you can run your business from a corner of your living room or your dining room table, it is not recommended. You'll feel much more productive and professional if you set up a permanent office space in a room or even a secluded corner of your home. Your clients will prefer the more professional setup, as well. You probably wouldn't feel comfortable meeting with your lawyer in her living room. Your clients will prefer to meet with you in a professional setting.

> **Smart Tip** Tip...
>
> For reasonably priced office furniture, check out www.furniture2go.com. This site offers an extensive assortment of office furniture as well as offering free shipping.

This space doesn't need to be expansive but it does need to be dedicated to your consultant business. Don't let the kids use your desk for homework. This is your space for your professional work.

In terms of furnishings, you will need an inexpensive desk or computer workstation, a comfortable office chair (preferably one that's ergonomic, since you'll be spending a great deal of time in it), and a sturdy two- or four-drawer file cabinet. You should also consider acquiring a bookcase so you can keep your reference materials conveniently at hand.

Office supply stores like Staples or Office Depot sell reasonably priced office furniture that will set you back as little as $200 for a desk, and $50 and up for a chair. A two-drawer letter-size file cabinet costs $25 to $100, while a four-shelf bookcase will cost around $70. In addition, you can often save a substantial amount of money on your desk or computer workstation by purchasing furniture that must be assembled (known as KD or "knock down") or by scouring the want ads for used furniture.

Swedish furniture seller IKEA also offers office furniture at low prices. A benefit to IKEA's furnishings is the design flair that this company offers it customers. IKEA offers high style at low prices.

Personal Computers

Some wedding consultants, like Donna H. in Austin, Texas, still like to keep their records the old-fashioned way, using a typewriter, paper spreadsheets, and a well-loved pen. But for most of us, personal computers are now pretty much a necessity for doing business. Desktop computers offer speed, convenience, and compatibility with other users. They use sophisticated, yet user-friendly software packages to crunch numbers, churn out your billing statements, figure your taxes, and connect you to the internet. Best of all, this efficiency and accuracy is now available at a cost that's reasonable enough even for a fledgling small-business owner—usually around $2,000 to $4,000 for a complete Pentium-based system that includes the hard drive, monitor, mouse, modem, and printer. With careful shopping, though, a computer can be found for closer to $1,500.

How Does a Computer Really Work?

If you haven't used a computer often or are intimidated by the prospect of buying a new one for your new business, read on. Kathie Flood, Senior Program Manager, Microsoft Games Studios, demystifies computers and offers some sound and straightforward advice for understanding these complicated machines.

○ *CPU: Central Processing Unit*. The CPU is your computer's brain, which can do thousands of different things per second. The speed of the CPU is measured in megahertz (MHz) or gigahertz (GHz) and should be no less than 1 or 1.2 GHz to run most common programs like Microsoft Office and Intuit QuickBooks. Many new computers have a dual processor, which is especially fast and efficient, i.e., improves battery life on a laptop.

○ *RAM: Random Access Memory*. RAM is your computer's short-term memory or virtual scratch pad. RAM is measured in megabytes (MB or megs, 1 million bytes) or gigabytes (GB or gigs, 1 billion bytes). More RAM enables your computer to run more complex programs. If your computer has at least 1 to 1.5 GB, you should be able to run most common programs smoothly and simultaneously.

○ *Hard Drive*. This is your computer's permanent storage space, which you can think of as long-term memory. Like RAM, hard-drive space is measured in megabytes (MB) or gigabytes (GB). However, because this is your computer's permanent storage space, you will need much more hard-drive space than RAM. You should have at least 40 to 60 GB to enable you to store the many photos, videos, and documents you will accumulate while running your business.

○ *CD or DVD Drive*. This is the device that plays CDs and/or DVDs. Many CD and DVD drives are also capable of writing to blank CDs and DVDs. Writeable CDs and DVDs are very useful for creating discs that contain documents, photos, and videos that are too big for e-mail or must be delivered via snail-mail or courier. You can also use writeable CDs and DVDs for small-scale backups.

○ *Operating System*. This is the program that enables you to tell your computer what to do. Most personal computers run Microsoft Windows as their operating system (Vista is the most current version), but there are others, such as Apple OS-X and Linux.

○ *Ethernet Port, Wireless Internet Card, and/or Modem*. These are all used to connect your computer to the outside world. An ethernet port is where you would plug a cable for direct network access. A wireless internet card also provides network access, but without a cable. A modem enables you to connect a network or to send a fax via a telephone line.

Dollar Stretcher

Many inexpensive printers—some under $100—are equipped with scanners. If you are not anticipating heavy use of a scanner, then buying a printer equipped with a scanner is a budget-wise choise.

If you have a little more money to spend, other useful add-ons include: a scanner (which will cost you in the range of $150 to $400, depending on the resolution) and a digital camera ($200 to $700), which allows you to download photographs directly to your computer. The camera will come in handy if there's some element of a wedding you'd like to preserve in your digital memory, such as a room layout or perhaps an especially unusual custom cake.

Software

Your software is the engine that makes your computer go. Most of the wedding consultants we spoke to use two basic software packages for conducting business:

Keep Track of Expenses

Just about anything you purchase for use in your business is deductible on your federal income taxes, provided you have the proper written documentation (like receipts and packing slips). The Section 179 expense deduction will currently allow you to deduct up to $20,000 a year for equipment costs including computers, office furniture, telecommunications equipment (phones, answering machines, telephone headsets), and fax machines. Other incidentals needed to run your business, like office supplies and professional journals and trade magazines, are also deductible. If any of these items are used for both business and pleasure (like your kids using the PC to research dinosaurs for a school project), you can only deduct the amount of time the computer is actually in service for the business. The IRS recommends keeping a log showing business versus personal usage.

Happily, other costs typically incurred by wedding consultants, including professional fees for attorneys and CPAs, advertising and marketing costs, business equipment repairs, voice mail, seminars required to improve business skills, trade show and conference fees, and bank fees, may be written off against the business taxes.

Check with your accountant for details and to make sure you are following all current tax laws. The IRS keeps a close eye on at-home businesses, particularly tracking if home offices are being used for business as well as pleasure. Don't fudge these numbers. It is in your best interest to have accurate numbers and a careful log of office space and use if the IRS comes calling.

Microsoft Office and Intuit QuickBooks. Microsoft Office, offered in both a standard and professional version, is a bundled package that includes word processing, spreadsheet, database management, e-mail, presentation, and scheduling programs. The 2007 version of this software ranges from about $400-600. QuickBooks is an easy-to-use accounting package that not only keeps your financial records but can manage your business checking account and print checks. The 2007 QuickBooks Pro version retails for around $200.

By now it should be obvious that attention to detail is one of the most important personal traits a wedding consultant must have. And one of the most important tools you'll need is a good planner to help you keep appointments and activities straight and on schedule. A Franklin planner or other notebook-style planner will work just fine. But if you're computer-proficient, you might consider using a PC-based calendar or scheduler program instead such as Microsoft Office.

Software for Wedding Consultants

Event Magic Pro (managing the details) and Room Magic Pro (room layout/floorplan) are software programs designed for wedding consultants. According to Kim Roberts of FrogWare, the company that develops this software, "Event Magic Pro has complete templates to guide you through the planning process—a big help when you are getting started using the software. The templates can all be customized so that you can tailor the software to meet your needs. A really nice unique feature is the Task Reminder list on the Home page. This is a list of all To Do items across all events—a master To Do list. The software also includes invoicing, timelines, checklists (for client and consultant), budget, pie charts, vendor comparisons, table assignments, wedding day agenda, wedding party report, menu selections, and more. You can email all of the information/reports. Room Magic Pro allows you to do the layout for the events (reception, rehearsal dinner, etc). The system does the initial layout for you based on the room dimensions, number of people attending, types of tables, and spacing requirements."

Event Magic Pro was designed by consultants. The design company, Frogware Software (frogwaresoftware.com) was approached by consultants and asked to develop the program. The first version was released in 1997. There are at least two releases of the software per year, all of which are driven by requests from our customers.

Event Magic Pro is $289 and Room Magic Pro is $69. There is a free demo on our web site—you can download and try the full program free for 30 days.

Tip...

Fax Machines

Although most new computer systems today come with a fax card already installed, you might find it more practical to have a separate fax machine on a dedicated telephone line. That way, your computer doesn't have to be running for you to send or receive a fax, plus today's fax machines do much more than just transmit or receive data—they also serve as scanners, copiers, and printers. A standard plain paper fax will cost $100 to $250, while a multi-function machine ranges from $250 to $800. If you opt to install your fax on a dedicated line, the installation fee will run $40 to $60; then there's a regular monthly service charge. But if you're on the phone a lot, which is a given for wedding consultants, a separate fax line makes good sense.

Telephone Land Lines and Answering Machines

Buy the best phone you can afford since you'll be using it constantly. A standard two-line speaker phone with auto-redial, memory dial, flashing lights, mute button, and other useful features will run $70 to $150, while a top-of-the-line model can cost $250 or more. A great source for high-quality phones is Hello Direct (see the Appendix), which carries the Polycom line of professional business telephones. And while you're at it, consider purchasing a phone with a headset for hands-free calling, so you can prevent the discomfort caused by cradling the receiver between your neck and shoulder.

Your answering machine is another must-have. No wedding consultant worth his or her salt can afford to miss a call during those times when they're away from the office. An answering machine is also useful when you're at the door signing for an express delivery, sitting down for a well-deserved (and possibly delayed) lunch, or shooing the kids out the door so you can do some work without interruption.

Today's answering machines often come as part of a cordless phone unit and have plenty of bells and whistles. One of the most useful features allows you to call in from a remote location and pick up your messages. A stand-alone answering machine may cost $40 to $150, while a cordless phone/answering machine combo will run $50 to nearly $200.

Cellular Phones

When this book was first published, cell phones were not the ubiquitous instrument they have now become. Simply put, every wedding consultant must have a cell phone at the ready. You will use it to follow up on details or make wedding arrangements while en route to appointments or events. If you play your cards right, you'll receive a brand-new phone at no charge at the time of service activation. Bear in mind, though, that a free phone often requires a fairly lengthy service contract, sometimes as long as two years. Sometimes it is preferable to buy the phone outright and forgo any onerous service agreement. You can expect to pay up to $200 for a reliable wireless phone.

Pagers

Pagers are a handy way to allow nervous brides and conscientious suppliers to contact you no matter where you are. (Keep in mind that this will include when you're in the bathroom, at your son's preschool graduation, in the frozen food section at the grocery store, etc.)

> **Tip...**
>
> **Smart Tip**
> Cell phones often prove invaluable the day of the ceremony. If your limousine driver hasn't appeared or the caterer is running late, you can touch base with these vendors easily and quickly. Store all of your vendors' phone numbers in your cell phone for easy one-touch dialing. Note: headsets are required in many states. Statistics show that more accidents are caused by cell phone use while driving than by drunken driving. Be safe and use a headset.

As with cellular phones, paging service providers often throw in a basic pager when you activate the service. If you prefer to buy one of those snazzy models that come in vibrant colors and have features like digital messaging, you can expect to shell out around $70. Typical costs for pager service are in Chapter 12.

Copy Machines

No one says you have to have a copy machine right in your office, especially when quickie print shops like Kinko's, Staples, or Speedy Printing are so conveniently located all around the country. But you can't beat the convenience of having your own copier right at your side, especially now that they cost as little as $500 to $800 for a standard business machine. Today's versatile models can reduce and enlarge, sort and collate, and produce double-sided copies. They use toner cartridges that are readily available from your local office supply store and sell for around $10 to $15.

> **Bright Idea**
> Play soft, tasteful music in the background when you record your answering machine message. Some classical selections that will give your message ambience: Canon in D by Pachelbel, or Air on a G String by Johann Sebastian Bach.

Check your local Yellow Pages directory for the names and numbers of dealers in your area.

Office Equipment and Supplies

Below are the office equipment and supplies costs for two hypothetical wedding consulting businesses: "Weddings by Jamie," a homebased company, and "Cherished Moments in Time," a start-up based in a commercial office space. The owner of "Weddings by Jamie" already had a basic computer system (not including a printer) and selected items to fit a limited start-up budget. The owner of "Cherished Moments in Time" decided to go with top-of-line equipment and furniture to outfit her office.

	Weddings by Jamie	Cherished Moments
Office equipment		
Computer, printer	$500	$4,000
Scanner	$0	$300
Software		
Microsoft Office	$600	$600
Intuit QuickBooks	$200	$200
Wedding software	$0	$70
Zip drive	$100	$200
Surge protector	$0	$35
UPS (or battery backup)	$0	$125
Digital camera	$0	$500
Fax machine	$0	$250
Copy machine	$0	$800
Phone	$70	$250
Cell phone	$100	$300
Voice mail	$6	$0
Answering machine	$0	$70
Postage meter/scale	$0	$25
Calculator	$15	$50
Office furniture		
Desk	$200	$600
Chair	$100	$250
File cabinet(s)	$100	$200
Bookcase	$0	$70
Office supplies		
Letterhead, envelopes, business cards	$200	$300
Miscellaneous supplies (pens, folders, etc.)	$50	$50
Computer/copier paper	$25	$50
Extra printer cartridges	$25	$80
Extra fax cartridges	$0	$80
Zip disks	$25	$50
3.5-inch floppy disks	$7	$12
Mouse pad	$0	$10
Total	**$2,323**	**$9,527**

Postage Meters and Internet Postage

Talk about a huge time-saver! Postage meters have eliminated those annoying trips to and from the post office (not to mention the long waits in line), and the process of licking and sticking stamps on envelopes and packages. That adhesive does contain calories, you know!

You actually have a couple of options when it comes to buying postage. You can lease a standard postage meter, which requires you to pay an annual mailing fee of about $100 and pay for postage upfront at the post office. Or you can forgo leasing the equipment altogether by buying your postage online from providers like Pitney Bowes (see Appendix). For a modest fee (usually no more than $4.95 per month) above the actual cost of the postage, you can download software that allows you to print your postage directly onto labels. You can charge the cost of the postage to any credit card.

Of course, you'll need a postal scale to make sure you're affixing enough postage to your outgoing mail. Some of the online companies will provide you with a postal scale free or for a nominal charge. Otherwise, you can expect to pay $10 to $25 for a mechanical scale (which is useful if you mail 1 to 12 items per day), or $50 to $200 for a digital scale (if you're sending 12 to 24 items per day). If you plan to send more than 24 items per day, or use priority or expedited mailing services on a regular basis, you should consider purchasing a programmable electronic scale, which will run $80 to $250.

Dollar Stretcher

For at-your-fingertips copy service, buy a computer printer which has a copy function. These hybrid printer/copiers sell at office supply stores and discount stores at prices starting under $100. These printers are not appropriate for high-volume print runs but are amazingly handy for smaller jobs.

Smart Tip

Customize your clients' stamps at zazzle.com. This web site enables customers to create their own stamps. For instance, couples might opt to use an icon from their wedding, perhaps the currently trendy monogram logo. Or brides- and grooms-to-be could elect to use their engagement photo on the stamp. This is a United States Postal Service approved site.

Office Supplies

You'll find that your costs in this category will be far more modest, but the office supply products you will buy are just as important to the functioning of your business as the equipment you purchase. Take your stationery and business cards, for example. These tools represent you and make a statement about you in your absence. For that reason, buy the best stationery you can afford. Print shops like Kinko's and office supply stores like Office Depot and Staples can whip up professional-looking coordinated stationery for you at a reasonable cost (about $80 for 250 one-color premium sheets, $85 for 250 envelopes, $35 for 250 business cards). There are also a number of mail order printing companies like Mark Art Productions (see Appendix) that can offer you a wide selection of standard paper, and printing styles and colors to choose from. As a general rule, you should stick with stationery in white, cream, or gray for an elegant, conservative look.

If you're operating on a real shoestring budget, you could purchase blank stationery materials from an office supply store and make your own on your office printer. This stationery runs under $6 for a package of 100 sheets of stationery, under $8 for 50 envelopes, and under $7 for 250 business cards. As far as other office supply costs go, you should figure on spending about $150, which will buy pens, pads, copy paper, file folders, and the like.

The Final Tally

If you kept an eye on all the estimated costs on the chart on page 61 as you read this chapter, you can get a pretty clear idea of how much capital it will take to cover equipment and supplies for your new business (use the worksheet on page 66 to figure your own expenses). Now take a look at the chart on page 65 for a tally of all the start-up costs it will take to get our two hypothetical wedding consultant businesses off the ground.

"Weddings by Jamie" is a homebased company with an office set up in the corner of the den. The owner financed the start-up with her personal credit cards. "Cherished Moments in Time" has a 500-square-foot office in a commercial building. This business has top-of-the-line equipment and furniture, and employs a contract person to help out with weddings, at a cost of $100 per wedding. "Weddings by Jamie" is projecting an annual gross income of $12,000 (12 weddings at $1,000 each), while the owner of "Cherished Moments in Time," which is located in an area where weddings average $2,500, expects to earn $37,500 (15 weddings at $2,500 each). Each business owner takes a percentage of the net profits as income.

> **Bright Idea**
> Raised letter printing (known as thermography) or gold foil stamping may cost a little more, but they add an elegant touch to your stationery and business cards. For the very best look, have your stationery printed on laid bond paper. It has the smoothest surface of all printing papers and produces the crispest printed images.

From the hypothetical expenses we've outlined in the chart on page 65, you can get an idea of what your start-up costs may look like. We've already covered the costs associated with market research (refer to Chapter 3); licenses and permits (Chapter 4); and hiring an attorney, and an accountant and buying insurance (Chapter 5). In Chapter 8, we'll look at the cost of certification, training, subscribing to publications, and joining professinal organizations. Advertising costs will be addressed in Chapter 9, and online service and web site design and hosting will be covered in Chapter 10. Tally up the start-up costs that you anticipate for your new business, using a form similar to the one we've provided in our example, or another of your choosing.

In addition to the costs listed here, you will also have ongoing monthly expenses once your business is up and running. See Chapter 12 for a discussion of these costs, as well as some advice on approaching bankers and obtaining financing.

Start-Up Expenses

Here are the start-up expenses for our two hypothetical wedding consultant businesses:

	Weddings by Jamie	Cherished Moments
Start-Up Expenses		
Rent (security deposit and first six months)	$0	$3,500
Office equipment, furniture, supplies	$2,273	$9,237
Business licenses	$150	$150
Phone (line installation)	$90	$115
Cell phone monthly charge	$50	$50
Utility deposits	$0	$150
Employee wages (first six months)	$0	$800
Start-up advertising	$100	$500
Legal services	$375	$525
Insurance (annual cost)	$125	$450
Market research	$500	$1,000
Certification/designation training	$340	$2,000
Membership dues (professional associations)	$150	$290
Publications (annual subscriptions)	$22	$47
Online service	$20	$20
Web site design	$800	$2,500
Web hosting	$20	$20
Subtotal	**$5,015**	**$21,354**
Miscellaneous expenses (add roughly 10% of total)	$500	$2,100
Total Start-Up Expenses	**$5,515**	**$23,454**

Your Office Equipment and Supplies

Office equipment	
Computer, printer	$
Scanner	
Software	
Microsoft Office	
Intuit QuickBooks	
Wedding software	
Zip drive	
Surge protector	
UPS (or battery backup)	
Digital camera	
Fax machine	
Copy machine	
Phone	
Cellular phone	
Voice mail	
Answering machine	
Postage meter/scale	
Calculator	
Office furniture	
Desk	
Chair	
File cabinet(s)	
Bookcase	
Office supplies	
Letterhead, envelopes, business cards	
Miscellaneous supplies (pens, folders, etc.)	
Computer/copier paper	
Extra printer cartridges	
Extra fax cartridges	
Zip disks	
3.5-inch floppy disks	
Mouse pad	
Total	$

7

Developing a
Vendor Network

One of the things that will make you valuable to your customer is your knowledge of the bridal industry. As a consultant, you are expected to be the font from which all knowledge about the industry flows. That means knowing things like which wedding gown styles or decorating schemes are in vogue and which are passé, or whether it's

Wedding News

On the big day, 62 percent of couples choose to have a flower girl, while 56 percent opt to have a ring bearer.

inspired or gauche to use silk flowers in the bride's bouquet.

All of the wedding consultants interviewed for this book agree that networking is the first and best way to determine who the best vendors are in your area.

Deborah McCoy, president of the American Academy of Wedding Professionals, puts it this way. "The best way to find vendors is to get referrals from recently married friends, family, business associates, and clients. The rule of thumb when it comes to finding vendors: Never . . . 'let your fingers do the walking.'

"When prospective consultants get referrals, they'll find that the same names pop up over and over—for good and for bad. It's then up to the consultant to build relationships with quality vendors."

But perhaps even more importantly, your clients will count on you to recommend reliable vendors that offer the best quality and value for their money. So it's your job to research bridal service providers in your target market area to find the best possible sources for the products or services you'll require. From this research, you should compile a list of preferred vendors you can either share with the bride during a consultation, or use yourself if you're in charge of all the planning.

Although this process can be rather time-consuming, it's essential for your own future success. Every time you recommend a vendor, you're putting your own reputation on the line, so you'll want to make sure your suppliers have impeccable credentials and excellent reputations.

How to Find the Best Providers

The easiest way to identify potential service providers is by asking friends and business acquaintances for recommendations. Other useful sources of information include the Internet, your local Yellow Pages, and the chamber of commerce. Do keep in mind McCoy's caveat about letting your fingers do the walking, meaning be cautious about your dependence on the Yellow Pages and phone. There is no sounder way to vet vendors than by networking and speaking with recently married couples as well as with other consultants in your area.

The Better Business Bureau can also be useful for helping you steer clear of businesses whose reputations are less than sterling. Check their web site, www.bbb.org, for more information.

In this initial fact-finding stage, don't limit yourself to locating a certain number of vendors. Rather, identify as many potential sources as possible so you'll have several to choose from when the time comes to make a recommendation to a bride. Keep in mind, too, that you should locate vendors in the low, medium, and high price ranges to accommodate all budgets.

Then once you have compiled your list of sources, pick up the phone and make appointments to see their facilities and products in person. Since business owners are generally pleased to grant you a personal interview and show off their services as a way to secure future business, those who balk should be removed from your list.

Go to each interview armed with a list of specific questions concerning the company's scope of services, prices, delivery schedules, terms, and so on. Don't rely on your memory to keep the details straight; eventually there will come a point when you've talked to or seen so many vendors you won't remember who's who. Instead, try creating a simple questionnaire or form on your home computer that you can fill out as you interview your potential sources. In addition to noting contact information, hours of operation, and location, be sure to ask for the company's web address.

"Business licenses, appropriate insurance, contracts, health permits for food providers, years in business, number of weddings worked on, and the ability to work well with other professionals should be at the top of your list when gathering information about vendors," says Robbi Ernst of June Wedding Inc.

Once your inspections are completed, evaluate providers in each category against one another and rank them based on quality, value, timely delivery, and so on. Finally, check their business references to verify both their reputations and their reliability. The top-ranked vendors become your preferred suppliers, although you can always add to this list as you hear about other promising vendors. Identifying numerous vendors in each category has another advantage: You'll always have someone prescreened and ready to go when your top choice is already booked.

As you get your business established, you should expect your supplier list to change. You'll probably add new vendors as well as remove those that don't live up to your expectations.

"I constantly shop for vendors to add to my library, so I have a large resource library that enables me to refer vendors based on the bride's preferences, personality, budget, and vendor availability," says Paula L., the wedding consultant in San Clemente, California.

Primary Vendors

As a wedding consultant, you will need to locate and coordinate with several types of vendors including reception facility managers, caterers, florists, DJs, photographers, limousine companies, and others.

The Reception Site

A substantial part of the bridal budget is devoted to the reception, which though once traditionally held in a banquet hall is now held at a wide variety of sites. When meeting with a reception site manager, be sure to inquire about the number of people the facility can accommodate, the cost per person, the number of hours the facility can be rented for, and the type of food it provides. Ask, too, about any restrictions there may be on the wedding party and their guests (such as a lack of handicapped facilities, a ban on smoking, or a ban on alcohol, a situation that you will find at some outdoor park sites).

Keep in mind that many banquet facilities offer full-service packages that include food, a wedding cake, a photographer, and even a videographer, so you might be required to select from the facility's own preferred vendor list. If you prefer to use your own sources, you should take your reception business elsewhere.

Finally, ask for permission to visit the facility during a wedding to observe the wait staff and the management in action, as well as the general operation of the business. You should also ask to sample any food provided for a typical wedding dinner.

These days, more and more bridal couples are choosing nontraditional sites for both their nuptials and receptions. According to Gerard Monaghan of the Association of Bridal Consultants, alternative locations like gardens are quite popular, as are luxury hotels where the ceremony and reception can be held in the same place. The trend to hold weddings in unusual locales also continues.

Receptive Receptions

Today's brides and grooms hold their receptions in a variety of venues, including:

○ Churches: 30%

○ Hotels: 20%

○ Country clubs: 20%

○ Fraternal halls, private homes, and other locations: 30%

As a wedding consultant, it is critical for you to know all of the likely—and sometimes unlikely—reception sites in your area. Remember to consider museums as well as historic homes, theaters, and restaurants. Ann Nola, of the Association of Certified Professional Wedding Consultants, says that the trend in California is toward having receptions at private estates.

"There are now so many scuba weddings that two companies are now manufacturing white wet suits," Monaghan says. "You name it, someone is doing it."

Deborah McCoy, of the American Academy of Wedding Professionals, agrees. "People always want to do something different! I recently read about a couple who wanted to have their wedding on an iceberg in New Zealand."

Contact your local chamber of commerce or county seat for a list of places (like restaurants and parks) that allow weddings at their facilities. Remember that a permit may be required, and there may be other restrictions.

Food, Glorious Food

Although many reception halls and other sites have their own caterers, it's still a good idea to establish your own network of caterers, especially for weddings in non-traditional settings. As with banquet facilities, you will want to talk to prospective catering sources about menus, specialties, and price ranges. You'll also want to find out if they can fulfill special requests (such as preparing kosher or vegetarian cuisine),

---

Food Trends

It is important for wedding consultants to stay on top—if not ahead!—of wedding trends. You can do this by networking with your vendors as well as by keeping up-to-date with trade and consumer publications. When it comes to catering trends, Leslie Bullock, a Manhattan-based caterer and owner of Herban Gourmet, offers these ideas:

○ Wedding guests don't want to sit down to a heavy meal—they are looking for small plates and small bites. Emphasis is on one-biters—nothing bigger than a tablespoon. Even crostinis and bruschetta are quarter- or half-dollar sized—at the largest.

○ Raw bars aren't just shrimp anymore. Instead, expect stone crab claws, lobster claws, and oysters opened to order.

○ Brides- and grooms-to-be are asking for more refined and elaborate stations—not the typical heavy buffet of the past.

○ Pretty and delicate are in, super size is out.

Prospective couples are looking for twists on old comfort foods. For instance, Herban Gourmet takes the classic twice-baked potato to new levels by using purple fingerling potatoes and adding truffle and pancetta to the mix.

and whether they provide linen, china, and glassware. Then ask permission to drop in on a function they're catering to sample the cuisine and observe the service.

Deborah McCoy recommends joining the National Association of Catering Executives (NACE) to meet caterers and other people in the wedding business. "I recommend meeting with other professionals and networking. One wonderful way is to join NACE. Wedding professionals of all types congregate at NACE meetings. It's a terrific way to meet people in the business and get your name out there. The point is to build professional relationships which will make your business grow."

Floral Arrangements

Flowers are an integral part of a wedding, so it's essential to select florists who can deliver floral designs that are both beautiful and innovative. Toomie Farris, American Institute of Floral Designers, American Association of Florists (AIFD, AAF), president of En Flora in Indianapolis, and an FTD Association Master Florist, says the best florists are the ones who take the time to understand the bride's vision for her special day, then translate that feeling into a coordinated floral display.

"I never let a bride or her consultant jump immediately into details like picking which bouquet she wants," Farris says. "It's more important to understand the entire event and the overall feel of the wedding, based on the bride's personal taste and the way she expresses herself."

Toward that end, when you interview florists, ask them about their approach to designing a coordinated wedding package. Although flowers make up a large chunk of the bridal budget (ranging from $500 to $1,000), a good florist can work wonders even on a budget. For example, Farris says a simple table arrangement consisting of a large monstera leaf sprayed with metallic paint and accented with bear grass and a few sprigs of fern has a high-style look, yet costs just $15 to create.

Florists can usually show you portfolios of their work to give you an idea of what they can do, but it's also a good idea to take a peek in the cooler to check the freshness of the floral product. Note particularly whether the water in the buckets is crystal clear, which indicates the flowers have been processed properly for maximum freshness.

Stat Fact

Chris Graze, owner of Thistles, a Flower Shop, in Connecticut, says that flowers are more than ever an essential element of the big day. "I've been in the business ten years and this has been my biggest yet for weddings." Her typical client spends in the $500 to $1,000 and up range. Graze enjoys her work with wedding consultants. "It is a joy to work with consultants. It is nice to have them as a buffer, to have them as the 'go to' person. They know the bride much better than we do."

The Language of Flowers

Chris Graze, owner of Thistles, a Flower Shop, says that roses remain a perennial favorite but finds that more and more brides are opting for natural, gardeny flowers, as well as focusing on more color than they once did. Garden flowers include fresh blossoms such as hydrangea, peony, colored mini-callas, and tulips. Bridemaids, on the other hand, often now have fewer colors in their bouquets since their dresses are more colorful than the brides'.

Some brides still ascribe to the charming Victorian practice of assigning meanings to blossoms. Here are the secret messages of love attached to some commonly used wedding flowers:

○ Alstoremeria: devotion
○ Baby's breath: pure of heart
○ Calla lily: beauty
○ Camellia: excellence, beauty
○ Carnation, white: perfect loveliness
○ Chrysanthemum, white: truth
○ Daisy: innocence
○ Delphinium: open heart and deep attachment
○ Gardenia: refinement
○ Lily of the Valley: return of happiness
○ Magnolia: magnificence
○ Lily, white: sweetness and purity
○ Orchid: love and beauty
○ Ranunculus: radiant with charm
○ Rose, red: I love you
○ Rose, white: purity and love
○ Rosebud, red: pure and lovely
○ Stephanotis: happiness in marriage
○ Tulip, red: love
○ Violet: faithfulness

Sources: FTD, USA Bride

And just as a side note: Balloons are definitely out. Farris says they're tacky and belong at baby showers, not elegant weddings.

Stat Fact

According to the American Disc Jockey Association, the rate for disc jockeys varies widely, with fees starting at $350 and rising to $3,500. The association reports an average rate of $1,200 per hour. Keep in mind, as a consultant, that the best price may not always result in the best DJ. As the adage goes, you get what you pay for. When advising clients, don't stint on the DJ.

The Sound of Music

Unless you are a real audiophile who keeps up with the latest tunes and musical trends, you should seek the help of a professional entertainment consultant to find bands that provide reception music. These consultants often have audition tapes on file to make the job of selecting musicians easier, but it's usually wiser to see the band perform live so you're not unpleasantly surprised by either the quality of their work or their physical appearance on the big day. Other sources for recommendations are hotel banquet managers, and anyone who works on site with bands, such as photographers and caterers, whose opinion you respect.

Ideally, your "play list" should consist of several bands that can pull off everything from Big Band music to rap. But it's more realistic to expect your musicians

DJ Considerations

When you are choosing a DJ, it's important to consider these questions:

○ Is the DJ insured? Does he have liability coverage? Ask for proof.

○ Will he play requests? Don't take it for granted that he will. Always ask.

○ What type of equipment does he have? Does he have backup equipment in case of equipment failure?

○ How much time is allowed for setup? This is critical because a tardy DJ can ruin the whole party.

○ How will the DJ dress? Again, don't take this for granted. You don't want a DJ showing up for a black tie function in blue jeans.

○ Will he agree to a written contract? If no, then choose another DJ. This contract protects him as well as your client.

○ Does he have an affiliation with a professional association?

Source: American Disc Jockey Association

to specialize in certain types of music. Generally speaking, a band that can play both rock and easy listening music will be suitable for most audiences.

A less expensive and potentially more versatile musical choice is a disk jockey. You can easily find DJs listed in the Yellow Pages under "Bands," "Music," or "Weddings," or you can ask friends and acquaintances for recommendations. There are also sites on the internet that can steer you toward a DJ. Three to try are 1-800-DISC JOCKEY at www.800dj.com; the American Disc Jockey Association at www.adja.org, phone (301) 705-5150; or wedj.com.

A good DJ will come prepared to handle special requests in many categories. Ask potential vendors for a list of the music he or she typically brings to a reception.

Say Cheese

Good photography is truly an art, so you'll want to screen prospective photographers very carefully. To locate photographers, try the Yellow Pages or an online search. The Professional Photographers of America Inc. at (888) 786-6277, or e-mail csc@ppa.com, can also provide you with potential sources, but keep in mind that these are just leads, not recommendations. Banquet facilities also may be able to refer you to experienced shutterbugs.

When reviewing a photographer's portfolio, note the settings and lighting conditions under which the snapshots were taken. Some photographers are more adept at interior photography than garden settings, for instance, just as some are more skilled at taking candids versus portraits. Each type of photographer has his or her place on your list.

You'll also want to assess the photographer's people skills, since he or she will be interacting constantly with the bride and groom. Look for someone who is professional, yet warm and friendly, and be sure to ask what he or she wears while working. Formal weddings require formal attire for vendors like the photographer, too.

Lights, Camera, Action!

As with photographers, you must view a videographer's work before adding him or her to your list of preferred suppliers. It's important to ascertain whether the sample footage you see was actually shot by that person or by

Dollar Stretcher

Consider having the photographer take only the formal photos, if budget is an issue. Let the guests take care of the casual shots by leaving disposable cameras on all of the reception tables. Another popular trend is to leave disposable video cameras on the tables so guests can take their own footage. When the newly married couple returns from their honeymoon, they have the treat of reviewing all of these casual, impromptu shots taken by their friends and family.

an assistant. It's a good idea to ask for recommendations from people who regularly use videographers, such as banquet facility managers and even other vendors. You want a professional who will be discreet and won't interfere with either the ceremony or reception. Above all, this means no bright lights and no pushy behavior to get just the right angle.

Finally, determine whether the videographer shoots just raw footage, or whether he or she will edit it and add an appropriate musical score. Obviously, the latter is more time-consuming and expensive, and requires more expertise.

> **Tip...**
>
> **Smart Tip**
> Always ensure that the venues allow videographers. Some churches do not allow videographers during the ceremony. Be sure to ask so that there will be no surprises on the big day.

Have Your Cake and Eat It, Too

Like all areas of wedding planning, cakes are becoming more sophisticated and better tasting, as well. No longer are brides- and grooms-to-be settling for a basic white cake. Instead, they are looking for unique cakes that represent who they are.

Locating a good baker certainly will be one of the tastier aspects of your vendor search. You can ask reputable caterers for leads, or contact the International Cake Exploration Societé at www.ices.org. Additional sources include the pastry chefs at upscale restaurants and banquet facilities themselves, which may even do the baking right on site. And, again, there is simply no better way to find good bakers than by networking and hearing by word-of-mouth just who makes the most interesting, unique, and delicious cakes.

> **Tip...**
>
> **Smart Tip**
> Cupcakes are becoming more and more popular as the cake of choice for today's couples. Beautifully decorated cupcakes are charming and just the right size for an individual serving. Also, centerpiece cakes have grown in popularity. Each table at the reception has its own centerpiece cake, enabling the cake to be served easily and negating the need for a floral centerpiece.

Pore over prospective vendors' portfolios of cake designs, then sample the offerings. Inquire, too, about the availability of cake accessories like toppers, pedestals, and fountains, all of which give the cake a custom look.

In some parts of the country (notably the South), a groom's cake is a charming tradition. The groom's cake is generally richer and denser than the bride's cake, and is often sliced and wrapped in ribbon-tied boxes so guests can carry pieces home to enjoy later. Another charming southern tradition calls for the baker to hide charms attached to ribbons in the cake.

Before the cake is cut, each bridesmaid pulls a ribbon to remove a small token like a four-leaf clover, which is a symbol of good luck, or a ring, which signifies the next to marry. Keep in mind, however, that some states have laws that prohibit the baking of inedible objects in cakes, so be sure to check state regulations before you offer such a service to a bride.

Cinderella's Coach

A bride's special day calls for the special transportation provided by a limousine service. Limousines are usually rented by the hour (with a three hour minimum) and often provide amenities like champagne. It goes without saying that it's important to locate a reputable limousine company because the safety of your clients and their families are at stake. In addition, Packy B., the wedding consultant in Ohio, warns that limousine companies are notorious for not holding up their end of the contract.

"A family member once used a limousine company that brought in an out-of-town driver to help with the summer crush of weddings," she says. "The driver didn't have a clue where he was going, plus it was 90 degrees that day, and the air conditioning

The Getaway

Lisa K., a Connecticut-based wedding consultant, has made use of some unusual means of transportation when designing weddings for her clients.

"I planned a wedding for a bride and groom who were getting married at a country club and then traveling to the beach for part of their reception. We used golf carts. We decorated them with loads of color and they looked wonderful. At another beach wedding, we used boats to convey the couple and guests back and forth. We decorated these, too, and they were beautiful and festive."

Keep your mind and options open to ideas such as those Lisa K. developed. Brides and grooms like their day to be unique and to reflect their personalities. By using these charming means of transport, Lisa K. conveyed the lifestyle of her clients.

Horse-drawn carriages and vintage trolleys also make charming conveyances for the bridal party. An added benefit: They can be used as a backdrop or "prop" for wedding photographs. As a special gift to the bride and groom, stock them with gourmet chocolates, champagne, and special hors d'oeuvres so they don't arrive at the reception hungry.

was broken. Obviously, this couple didn't ask for any referrals from their sister-in-law, the wedding consultant!"

To avoid this kind of problem, contact the National Limousine Association at (800) 652-7007 or www.limo.org for a list of preferred service providers. You should actually inspect the company's vehicles to assess their general condition, upkeep, and size.

Make sure that a contract is signed and be sure to interview references given to you by the limousine companies with whom you choose to work.

Certification and
Professional
Development

Every consultant interviewed for this guide stressed the importance of training and education as two of the best paths toward developing a successful wedding consultant business. As Deborah McCoy, president of the American Academy of Wedding Professionals, a certification program, succinctly says, "It is critical that anyone embarking

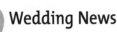

Wedding News

Although roses remain the number-one flower in many U.S. markets, New York City brides give peonies the nod for their number-one wedding flower pick. Beginning with number ten, New York City brides, according to *New York* magazine, choose these flowers for their nuptial bouquets: flowering branches, dahlias, gardenias, hydrangea, ranunculi, orchids, calla lilies, garden roses, tulips, and peonies.

on this career should become educated and certified."

Yet, if you flip open the course catalog for any major university in the United States, you'll see degree programs that teach people a wide variety of skills, including how to package and move objects, perform open heart surgery, and run corporations. What you won't find there is a curriculum that specifically teaches a person how to become a wedding consultant.

Yet wedding consultants need many of the same business skills that other professionals routinely acquire at universities and colleges. These are skills they use every day for project management, personnel administration, financial planning, even logistics. That's why, over the years, the denizens of the wedding consultant industry have created their own professional certification and training programs. No doubt this was done in part to combat the misconception that wedding consultants were merely bored housewives or terminally perky people who planned their own weddings and loved the experience so much they just had to start businesses of their own.

"These people are 'dabblers' who simply appropriate the title of 'professional,'" says Robbi Ernst III, president and founder of June Wedding Inc. "Many of today's consultants have experience in wedding-related businesses such as catering or event planning, and it's that kind of experience that makes them successful wedding consultants."

Just as you wouldn't choose a lawyer who hadn't passed the bar or a doctor who hadn't completed his residency, more and more brides- and grooms-to-be are thoroughly checking a wedding consultant's background. These couples are considering consultants' educations as well as certification and professional affiliations when making a decision about who should help plan this all-important day.

While a college business degree is definitely a plus for anyone planning to start a small business, it's not an absolute necessity. After all, it's

Dollar Stretcher

Many of the wedding consulting associations offer a wide range of membership benefits, including the use of the organization's logo in literature and advertising, merchant credit card acceptance programs, discounts on bridal show booth space, group rates on insurance, and even discounts on rental cars.

not uncommon for business owners of all kinds to hire professionals like accountants or public relations officers to handle tasks they don't have experience with. You can do the same thing. In the meantime, your own common sense and innate intelligence can help to make you successful in the bridal consulting industry. Then you can take professional development courses and certifications to fill in any gaps in your knowledge.

As Robbi Ernst of June Wedding, Inc., points out, choosing to become certified can help a consultant to realize profits more quickly. "A wedding consultant certification program can teach a person new to the business valuable knowledge that it would otherwise take two, even three years of experience. Otherwise, profits are going to take longer to be realized.

> **Smart Tip** Tip...
>
> When choosing a certification program, Deborah McCoy, President of the American Academy of Wedding Professionals, offers this tip: "When you're trying to decide on a wedding consultant course, the first thing to do is to ask who wrote it. *Make sure that the author is a bona fide wedding planner who plans weddings for a living.* You don't want to take a course from someone who only writes about weddings. You need a hands-on professional to teach you the ropes."

"We have done surveys that show that wedding consultants who are formally trained and certified can get higher fees from the onset of their business if they are professional and know what they're doing. My strongest advice to anyone starting in this business is to seek out the best and most competent professional training in the industry. The experts can teach you how not to make the mistakes they made, which can save you a small fortune."

"The wedding consultant is the expert, and if you are going to be an expert in this industry, you have to know as much as possible on all levels," says Packy B., the wedding consultant in Broadview Heights, Ohio. "I suggest you take as many courses as you can afford."

Certification Success

Robbi Ernst, president of June Wedding Inc. (JWI), knows the value of wedding consultant education and certification, having been a wedding consultant himself for three decades.

"The information that's imparted in these courses is information that really works in real life situations," Ernst says. "An advantage of JWI's course is that it's not just a correspondence course. There are three telephone consultations in the program so the student has genuine human interaction with an instructor and can ask questions or ask for clarification right away rather than having to wait for an e-mail or a written

Smart Tip

Tip...

Community colleges often will allow business entrepreneurs to take a few classes without having to enroll in a formal degree program. Community college tuition rates are usually very reasonable. It's sometimes even possible to audit a class for no grade (although this also means your classwork won't be evaluated). Opt for entry-level management and accounting classes to help hone your business skills. Or, choose communication or marketing classes to help you grow your wedding consultant business.

critique sent through the mail. They can also get ongoing follow-up technical support and help at no charge as long as they remain a member in good standing."

Ernst points out that the wedding industry has changed significantly over the years, so the need for professional development has changed, too. "When I started out in this industry, wedding consultants were not much more than people who sold invitations, did calligraphy, wrapped almonds in tulle, and such," he says. "I founded JWI because I had a different vision. I saw the need for a true professional and intelligent consultant who knew how to give good guidance to a bride. What the JWI home-study course has done for the industry is to create consistency. You can call a JWI-trained and certified consultant in Boise, Chicago, New York, or Dallas and get a similar professional response from each of them."

Choosing the Right Program

Certification programs run the gamut, from three-day seminars to years-long courses. Some involve phone consultations while others include classes presented via video. Consider these guidelines when selecting a certification program:

- *Consider lifestyle.* If you are the mother of young children, an extensive certification program may not work for you. Perhaps, a weekend seminar, addressing the basics of wedding consulting is more appropriate. Conversely, if you are an empty-nester with more time on your hands, then consider a more indepth program.

- *Consider cost.* For most of us, cost will also be a determining factor. Some certification courses offer very inexpensive ($300 and up) introductory seminars and certification programs. On the other end of the spectrum, some intensive training programs can run into the tens of thousands of dollars.

- *Consider credentials.* As you consider certification programs, take time to carefully consider the association's credentials. Are there testimonials on the web site attesting to the association's strong certification program? Are you able to contact wedding professionals who have taken the course and ask for their thoughts and feedback? Who wrote the course materials? Make sure that a wedding consultant—not an event planner—wrote the materials.

- *Consider benefits.* Will you be listed on the association's web site after you've completed your certification? This is a wonderful way to promote and network your business. Is there continuing guidance and assistance? Make sure that the association offers ongoing support, free of charge, as long as you maintain your membership. Does the association offer meetings or conferences? Does the association offer chat rooms? Look at the association as not just a means to certification but also as an opportunity to join a network of wedding professionals. Make sure that the association offers this all-important benefit.

- *Consider requirements.* Some certification programs require more experience than others. For instance, says Ann Nola, Director, Association of Certified Professional Wedding Consultants, this association will not certify those without experience. "I firmly do not believe in giving anyone a certification if they have no experience. Some associations do not require this experience. With these groups, all you need to do is take their course and then upon completion you get a certificate saying you're certified. At ACPWC, we believe that in order to be certified, you need experience." This experience includes planning weddings under the association's guidance and then gathering letters of recommendation.

- *Consider course offerings.* Some certification programs are focused entirely on the business aspects of wedding consulting—maintaining budgets, creating financial worksheets, billing, etc. Other associations offer courses dealing with some of the creative aspects of the business, such as design and color selection. Consider which areas you need to enhance. Perhaps, you've never managed to balance your own checkbook! Then, you should choose a certification program that emphasizes the business basics since you will need to have a solid financial foundation to successfully run your business.

As you develop your business, you will have to make decisions regarding continuing education and certification programs. If you live in a rural area and are the only wedding consultant for miles around, certification may not be necessary. Instead, you will rely on good word of mouth. Remember, you're only as good as your last event.

For wedding consultants in more urban areas facing stiffer competition, certification may be an absolute essential as savvy brides- and grooms-to-be increasingly tend to choose consultants with professional certifications.

Industry Publications

Another way to get educated and stay current on news, information, events, and trends in the wedding industry is by subscribing to publications that serve both the consultant and the consumer. Here's a brief rundown on some of the best-known publications that can keep you plugged into this ever-changing industry.

Trade Publications

- *Vows magazine.* This publication, which comes out six times a year, is available only to the bridal trade and provides information that runs the gamut from industry trends to customer service and business techniques. The subscription cost is $25 per year.

Consumer Publications

- *Bride Again.* An online publication for "encore" brides over the age of 30 whose readership has a median household income of $61,500 per year. Second-time brides tend to be older and established in a career, which makes them prime prospects for wedding consulting services. Visit www.brideagain.com.

- *Bride's Magazine.* One of the two premier wedding guides for brides that's instantly recognizable thanks to its doorstop-sized issues, some of which have more than 1,000 pages. This magazine is published six times a year. The subscription price is $11.97, or two years for $21.97. It's a must read. In addition, the publication has a web site called WeddingChannel.com that features the best of the magazine.

- *Modern Bride.* The other heavy hitter in the consumer bridal market. It's published six times a year. Like its competitor, it emphasizes the romantic fantasy of weddings, yet also offers brides useful tips on wedding planning, beauty, fashion and style, relationships, and other provocative issues. This magazine is another must for the wedding consultant because it's what your customer is reading. A one-year subscription is $9.95. *Modern Bride* also publishes 16 state editions twice a year (with names like *Michigan Bride*) that have specialized coverage of every aspect of bridal planning in that state.

- *Expo.* Wedding consultants often find general event planning publications helpful as idea-starters and information wellsprings. *Expo* is useful for wedding consultants because it taps into tradeshow topics of importance to exhibitors. A one-year subscription is $48.

- *Exhibitor Magazine.* This publication also serves trade show and event marketing professionals. A one-year subscription to this magazine costs $68.

9

Marketing Your Growing Business

As you grow and develop your company, marketing your skills and commitment will become increasingly important. We've all heard the catch phrases such as "We love to see you smile," "I can't believe I ate the whole thing," and "Moving at the speed of life."

They're all memorable advertising slogans created to increase awareness and name recognition for a specific product. They are all part of these companies' branding processes. Although you don't have to dream up a catchy tagline or jingle that people will be humming from coast to coast, you do need to devise a carefully crafted advertising plan that can help boost your business and create a positive image.

Many of the wedding consultants we spoke to rely on word-of-mouth (WOM) advertising and Yellow Pages listings as the basis of their advertising efforts. Often, these strategies alone are enough to fill a consultant's calendar comfortably. But there are many other easy and inexpensive things you can try that you may find especially effective for your particular region and situation. In this chapter, we'll examine the full range of techniques you can use to market your business and make it the top-of-mind choice for brides who are looking for a creative and responsive wedding consultant.

Your Marketing Plan

Before you start dropping dollars on advertising of any kind, it's wise to create a basic marketing plan. This plan doesn't have to be complicated, but it should be detailed enough to serve as a roadmap that keeps your business on track and your marketing efforts on target. In addition, it should be updated periodically as market conditions change so you are always in touch with the needs of your customers.

Your marketing plan can be a part of the business plan you've already written. (Refer to Chapter 4 for information about business plans.) It should describe your target market and the competitive environment you are operating in (this is where your market research comes in—refer to Chapter 3), as well as address how you're going to make your customers aware of your business. Information relating to pricing, industry trends, and advertising also has a place in your marketing plan.

SWOT Analysis

An integral part of the marketing plan is your SWOT analysis. SWOT stands for:

- *Strengths*. Characteristics that make you special and set you apart from the competition. Really consider this area because you have to differentiate your consultant work from your competitors, especially if you are in an urban area and have lots of competition. Really consider why your services are better and special.

- *Weaknesses.* Things you need to overcome or work on that your competitors could take advantage of. Again, be honest and specifically pinpoint areas that need work. Don't be vague. For instance, don't simply say, "I want to be more patient." Instead, make specific goals. For instance, "I will take more time with vendors and carefully listen to them," is a more directed statement.

- *Opportunities.* Anything you can do that might benefit your business either now or in the future. Are there new venues in your area that might be open to wedding receptions, for instance?

- *Threats.* Anything that can harm your business. Have economic conditions in your area taken a nose dive? Are there new wedding consultants hanging out their shingles?

Putting these characteristics on paper will give you a snapshot of your business's prospects.

SWOT Analysis

The following chart is an example of what a SWOT analysis might look like for a new wedding consultant business that will be operating in a medium-sized market of at least 25,000 people.

Strengths

- ❑ My strong business background (crucial expertise in business development!).
- ❑ My experience with event planning for conventions with 1,000 attendees.
- ❑ My strong communication skills (including writing).

Weaknesses

- ❑ No experience with advertising, marketing.
- ❑ Can't travel outside of immediate area because of husband's work schedule and child-care needs.

Opportunities

- ❑ No other consultants located within five-mile radius.
- ❑ New condo community nearly completed is geared toward middle-aged empty nesters that may have marriage-age offspring.

Threats

- ❑ Banquet facility at corner of Cleophus Avenue and Ferris has just added a wedding consulting package.
- ❑ Rumors that city is changing zoning to disallow homebased businesses.

▲

Examinie the SWOT analysis on the previous page to see what one might look like for a new wedding consultant in a medium-sized market of at least 25,000 people. Try creating your own SWOT analysis using the blank form we've provided below. You can also use the SWOT approach to analyze the strengths and weaknesses of your competition to see how you stack up against them. Once you've created your SWOT analysis, refer to it often as a guide for addressing the weaknesses you've identified and as a benchmark against which you can judge your successes.

Smart Tip

When writing your marketing plan, think about every time you'll interact with your customers. This includes everything from personal contact during consultations, through e-mail, and even the invoices you'll send. Each contact should be considered to be a potential marketing opportunity.

Tip...

Julia K., the wedding consultant in Oak Point, Texas, found out firsthand the benefit of doing a SWOT analysis. "We wrote a formal marketing plan using a SWOT

SWOT Analysis Worksheet

Use the following worksheet to do a SWOT analysis for your own business.

Strengths

1. _____
2. _____
3. _____

Weaknesses

1. _____
2. _____
3. _____

Opportunities

1. _____
2. _____
3. _____

Threats

1. _____
2. _____
3. _____

analysis because we wanted to make sure that the business was going to be profitable considering that I was going to make it replace my current income and supplement my partner's income," she says. "What we determined from the analysis and market research was that, had we done what we originally intended, we would have failed miserably. I can say that with all confidence because there is another consultant doing what we were going to do and she is failing.

"What we learned was that our market area was too small and too far removed from the places where the big money was being spent. We were planning to begin in a small town and move toward Dallas. Instead, we took a little longer to get our ducks in a row and began right in the heart of Dallas."

The Art of Advertising

Another important part of your marketing plan is your promotion strategy. Every wedding consultant, from the "one-man band" who coordinates just a handful of weddings annually to the person who needs a large staff to help handle the workload, must advertise to get new business.

The types of advertising that are most effective for wedding consultants include Yellow Pages advertising, magazine ads, brochures, business cards, and word-of-mouth. Each method is discussed below.

Advertising in the Phone Book

Without exception, the wedding consultants who we spoke to said that their Yellow Pages ad was a low-maintenance, low-cost workhorse that returned great value for their advertising dollar. There are two types of ads to choose from. The first is the line ad, which is the basic listing that's published under a heading like "Wedding Consultants" or "Wedding Services." Line ads normally contain only the business name, address, and telephone number, and are provided to you free of charge when you turn on your phone service. These days, some directories will also list your web address for an additional fee, which is usually worth the cost.

Some directories also allow you to place an expanded line ad that gives you room for additional information. One wedding consultant in the Southwest pays a modest $60 a month for her one-by-one-inch in-column ad. She feels the money is well spent and plans to add color for an additional charge to give it more emphasis.

The second type of ad is the display ad. It's usually boxed and is much larger than a line ad. As a result, a display ad can contain far more copy, including details about the services you offer, your hours of operation, and even a piece of clip art that relates to your business—like a bridal bouquet or a pair of stylized wedding bells. Display ads

Five Biggest Mistakes

Barbara Koch, author of *Profitable Yellow Pages*, says you can make your display ads more effective by avoiding these common mistakes:

1. Selling the category, not your business. If a bride opens the phone book to the wedding consultant listings, she doesn't have to be convinced that she should hire a consultant. So sell yourself in your ad to make her choose you over the others who are listed. Emphasize what's special about your business and tell her something she needs to know that sets you apart from your competition.

2. Selling products, not benefits. Of course you handle catering, flowers, and other wedding day services. So instead, emphasize what makes your business special and how in turn you can make the bride's day special.

3. Emphasizing nothing. This has more to do with the appearance of the ad than the content. If everything in the ad is visually the same (same typeface, same type size, etc.), nothing seems important. At the very least, use a larger type size for your header, and consider adding color to make the ad stand out.

4. Using tired phrases. Terms like "full service," "number one," and "highest quality" are so overused they've lost their meaning. Instead, use action verbs and powerful language, like "making dreams come true," to convey your message.

5. Using your business name as your header. Putting your company name at the top of the ad doesn't grab attention or tell the reader anything about your business.

are sold by the column width and the depth in inches. Most directories have their own standard sizes, so you'll have to inquire about both the size and the cost.

Often, a line ad is enough to attract calls from interested brides, as Donna H., the wedding consultant in Austin, Texas, can attest. She has coordinated nearly 8,500 weddings in a career that has spanned 25 years and does little advertising outside of her line ad. But if you do decide to buy a display ad, examine the directory listings carefully to make sure there's an appropriate category heading that brides can find easily.

You might think that placing a display ad when everyone else has a line ad would be a

Dollar Stretcher

Always check to see if your competition places display ads. If not, that's a pretty strong indication that it's not necessary to spend the money to attract callers.

great way to grab attention. But that's not necessarily the case, according to Barbara Koch, author of Profitable Yellow Pages.

"Many small business owners buy more ad space than they need," Koch says. "Yellow Pages ads are effective because advertisers have a captive audience who have already made a decision to buy. But that's also what makes it unnecessary to buy a display ad in most cases. The real role of your ad is to get the customer to choose you over someone else, and factors like your location may be what actually causes them to call you."

Overall, Yellow Pages advertising is a cost-effective technique for attracting business. But it does have a few disadvantages. For instance, let's say your local directory is published in April, but you didn't start your business until May. A full year will go by before your ad ever appears in the directory. On the other hand, Directory Assistance callers will be able to request your telephone number, but only if they know the exact name of your business.

Another disadvantage is that if the name of your business begins with a letter at the end of the alphabet, you'll be at the bottom of the list of wedding consultants. If the list isn't very long, that isn't much cause for concern. But if you're operating in a large city that has many wedding consultants, you could be overlooked by starry-eyed, busy brides.

A third disadvantage is that unless you buy a big display ad, your ad may be placed in the gutter, which is the space formed by the adjoining pages in the book. This can make it harder for customers to find your ad, especially if the directory is large and doesn't lie fully flat when opened. Unfortunately, you have no control over the placement of your ad in the directory. The best you can hope for is that the design of your ad or the use of color will make it stand out.

To place a Yellow Pages ad, or for more information, call the publisher of the directory you wish to display in.

Magazine Display Ads

In magazine publishing, a 60/40 advertising-to-editorial ratio is considered the Holy Grail, which means there's plenty of room for your paid advertisement in practically any magazine you choose to advertise in.

Most wedding consultants interviewed for this book found these ads to be much less effective than advertising in the Yellow Pages.

"Big, splashy ads in these publications are expensive, and small ads—which are still expensive—are hardly worth the money since they seldom catch the attention of the reader. In my 30 years in this business, I learned that advertising in these magazines is, for the most part, not effective in bringing in clients," says Robbi Ernst III of June Wedding, Inc.

It's best to advertise only in consumer publications that cater specifically to brides since, at any given time, only 1 percent of the population is considering marriage. The "biggies" in the bridal industry are *Bride's* and *Modern Bride*. In addition, many cities have their own monthly bridal magazines, which are excellent vehicles for your ad. (One to try: *Modern Bride*, which publishes a regional magazine in numerous U.S. markets.)

Advertising in these publications can be expensive. To get the best possible rate, run what's known as a schedule of ads, since the per-insertion rate is reduced when you repeat the ad over a set period of time. Another bonus: Studies show that ads that are repeated regularly tend to generate the most interest among consumers. It's really not beneficial to advertise only when you need business, so save your money if you can only afford one or two insertions.

If you have some imagination and access to a publishing software program like InDesign, you can try your hand at designing your own ad. But since you'll be spending a lot of money running that ad, which has the potential of being seen by thousands of readers, you probably should have it professionally designed. You don't have to go to a big advertising agency to get the job done. It's far more cost-effective to find a freelance artist through your local Yellow Pages, professional advertising association, or university art department. Even the internet can be a viable source. Using a search engine, type in keywords like "commercial artist" or "graphic designer" to locate prospects.

Like your Yellow Pages display ad, your magazine print ad should be eye-catching and informative. Focus on the unique things your business does best, and be sure to give full contact information, including your telephone number (and toll-free number, if applicable), and your web site and e-mail addresses. You should develop a special logo for use in your ad, as well as on your stationery and business cards and any other marketing materials. This will help cement your image in clients' minds. Think of those famous golden arches. They symbolize fast food for many of us. It's best not to use a logo from your art or word processing program's clip art library. Chances are, someone else is already using that clip art diamond ring or embracing couple in his or her advertising. Always go for a custom-designed logo that reflects your personal taste and style.

Incidentally, newsletters also often accept advertising at a cost that's considerably less than that of a magazine ad. If your regional bridal newsletter accepts advertising, it could be a very good place to spend your marketing dollars.

Smart Tip

Many cinema multiplexes offer on-screen advertising spots before the featured film. These spots are a prime opportunity to reach out to target your local audience. Call your local cineplex and ask to talk to the advertising representative.

Brochures

A brochure is a great tool for reaching brides-to-be in the places they're likely to frequent, like bridal shops, bakeries that specialize in wedding cakes, photographers studios, caterers, and so on. The cover should prominently feature your company name and have your own, unique logo.

Other elements the brochure should include are:

- A detailed list of your services

- Testimonials from satisfied customers ("ABC Bridal made my wedding a wonderful day to remember!"—Constance Zebracki, Detroit Lakes, Minnesota)

- Testimonials from vendors ("I enjoyed working with ABC bridal. They made my job so much easier!"—An Affair to Remember Catering)

- Contact information (your address, phone number, fax number, e-mail address, web site address)

Brochures can take many forms. The most common are the two- and three-panel brochures that, when folded, will fit into a number ten envelope. Stationery and office supply stores sell brochure stationery and envelopes that can be used in a laser or ink jet printer. But for a more professional look, have your brochures designed by a professional artist and printed on a high quality paper stock to reflect the high quality your customers can expect from your business. Again, calling on an old adage, "you have to spend money to make money." Spending money to produce a classy, tasteful, luxe feeling brochure will benefit your growing business.

Your brochure is a powerful marketing tool that works for you day or night, even when you're not there. For this reason, you'll want to distribute it widely. Start by making arrangements with local bridal and florist shops to display your brochure, either for a small fee or a promise to recommend them to the brides who engage your services. Be sure to provide a small literature holder with the brochures to keep them neat and tidy on the counter. (These acrylic racks are available for about $2.99 each through office supply stores like Office Max and Staples.)

You'll also want to consider mailing your brochure to prospective brides in the geographical area you serve. Many publications sell their mailing lists and can segment the names by zip code or other criteria you choose. Refer to Chapter 3 for more information on how to find and purchase mailing lists.

> **Tip...**
>
> **Smart Tip**
>
> Don't get caught short-handed. Always carry a supply of brochures in your briefcase so you'll always have one available to hand out with your business card when any conversation turns to matters matrimonial.

Smart Tip

Many wedding consultants are offering a tri-fold business card when they market their businesses. These business cards retain the small trim size of a traditional business card—so can still be easily tucked into a wallet—but because they are made up of three folded sections, the consultants are able to include more information and graphics describing their unique businesses.

Regional bridal shows often compile their own mailing lists and make them available for sale. These are called "hot lists," or compilations of likely buyers. A caveat, though: these likely buyers are looking for wedding vendors at the bridal shows, e.g., photographers, caterers, and the like. As the wedding consultants interviewed for this book point out, those attending bridal shows often do so because they feel they cannot afford a consultant. These couples hope to find all of their vendors at the bridal show thus negating the need to hire a consultant.

If you do decide to buy a list of bridal show attendees, contact the show's public relations office a few weeks after the show (to make sure they have time to finalize their list) to determine whether you will be allowed to buy it.

Business Cards

Here's a great way to advertise at a very low cost. Your business card is not only your calling card; it reminds a prospective bride, or her parent(s), that you're only a phone call or an e-mail away. As a result, you should distribute your card freely wherever you go. The sole exception: Don't ever give out business cards at a wedding you are coordinating, unless you are specifically asked for one. There's nothing less professional or tackier than placing a neat little pile of business cards on the cake table or—horrors!—handing out unsolicited cards to the unmarried guests in attendance.

One note: while a script typeface may look elegant, avoid using too much of it on your cards. Some people find it difficult to read.

Business cards are usually designed to match your business stationery, and it's generally more cost-effective to print the whole order at the same time. As mentioned in Chapter 6, you should use the highest quality paper stock you can afford, as well as thermographic printing, since these give your printed materials an expensive look that reflects well on your business.

Finally, as with all of your marketing products, be sure to feature your logo prominently on your business cards. It is vital that your logo become imprinted on your clients' memories.

Word-of-Mouth Advertisting

Whoever said there's no such thing as a free lunch must have overlooked word-of-mouth (WOM) advertising. Not only is the price right, but WOM praise is one of the most powerful advertising vehicles you have at your disposal. One of its major advantages is that you often don't have to do anything special to garner this kind of freebie publicity. All you must do is perform your job to the best of your ability, and people will talk favorably about you and your willingness to do whatever it takes to satisfy the customer.

Alexander Hiam, author of *Marketing for Dummies* (1997, IDG Books Worldwide Inc.), says the key to getting good WOM is influencing what your customers say about you. You can do this in a number of ways. Some wedding consultants call their clients a few weeks after the wedding to get feedback and verify their satisfaction. Doing this projects a positive image of you and your company because it's so rare for businesspeople in service industries to follow up after the sale. You might also get a referral or two from the satisfied bride during the conversation, which you can turn into a WOM opportunity by using her name when you call the person to whom she referred you.

Spread the Word

According to Robbi Ernst, of June Wedding, Inc., wedding consultants simply can't overestimate the power of word or mouth marketing.

Obviously, word of mouth is a considerably high means of getting clients. That alone should be impetus for wedding consultants to make certain that every wedding they produce is a first class wedding, no matter how limited the budget is. I have found through the years that wedding consultants, especially new ones, tend to become impatient when they get phone calls from prospective clients. The attitude seems to be that it is such a nuisance when they get a sense that the caller is 'shopping around' or 'trying to get free advice.' I take a different stand. I feel that any time one can do something for someone else, even if the person is not going to hire me because of her financial situation, that I should do so. If nothing else, that bride is more likely to tell someone she had a good experience in talking with me, and what better way to get free advertising? Besides, the alternative to that is for her to tell someone that I was rude or impatient or something else negative about my company.

Another way to influence WOM is by doing something positive and visible in your community or on the wedding business circuit. For example, you could host a complimentary hour-long, do-it-yourself wedding workshop for low-income brides and invite the local media to attend. Any coverage you get is bound to focus not only on your benevolence, but also on the services you offer. That can lead to new business.

A third way to influence WOM is by becoming involved in local business organizations, like Rotary International or the chamber of commerce. As you may know, many people have the perception that wedding consultants are "dabblers," who like to attend weddings and have turned that interest into a little side business. Although thankfully this perception is changing, you can establish yourself as a professional by networking at meetings of these local organizations. The members, in turn, are likely to use your services themselves, or recommend you to others in need of a wedding coordinator.

The Power of
the Internet

E ven a few short years ago, it was possible to grow a business without being reliant on the internet. This is absolutely no longer the case. Simply put, the internet brings the whole globe to your fingertips. And, this awesome global reach is accessible 24/7.

Wedding News

According to Forbes.com research, it is estimated that upwards of $16.8 billion could be spent on gay marriage ceremonies.

As you develop your business, you will rely on the internet to find supplies, to network, and to market your company. In a word, having access to the internet is as essential to your business as owning a phone. It is simply mandatory.

As Nancy Tucker of Coordinators' Corner puts it, "A web site is absolutely essential. Today's bride is very net savvy and is shopping for her wedding day and night."

Along with having 24/7 access, you will have access to hundreds of millions of internet users from around the globe. According to comScore, 700 million people use the internet. There are 152 million internet users in the United States alone.

All this accessibility opens the door to new and exciting business opportunities for you. It also means that, as a fledgling wedding consultant, you cannot overlook the power of the internet, both as a resource for your own business and as an electronic pathway for your customers. That bears repeating. You must be online these days because consumers have become so used to having information whenever they want it. Many of these consumers will surf the net to find answers and leads to products and services. So if you're not out there when they're looking, they definitely will go somewhere else.

"I get a lot of hits on my web site, and probably 50 percent of my business comes from those leads," says Packy B., the wedding consultant in Ohio. "This percentage is high and probably should not be expected by most wedding consultants. It happens because I have links from some very high traffic areas, and I keep track of and update them whenever I make any changes."

This chapter will not teach you the basics of surfing the web. We will assume that you know how to log onto an ISP, use a search engine, and send and retrieve e-mail. Instead, we will discuss the ways you can use the internet to help you run your business and capture new customers at the same time. But if by chance you're internet illiterate, you must learn to use this valuable resource right away. Community colleges, local libraries, and adult education programs are excellent places to learn about this amazing tool. There are also many books and software packages on the market that can walk you through the basics of e-mail, surfing, and web site development.

Now, let's start surfing . . .

An Amazing Resource

One of the most important uses you'll have for the internet is as a resource. As you establish your business, you can turn to the web for everything from advice on sticky business matters, like collections problems, to locating vendors that can provide services your brides will need. You can do market research and investigate local zoning ordinances and tax implications. And you can accomplish all of this any time of the day or night, and all without leaving the comfort of your home office.

You can also find small business opportunities and advice on the internet. Although there are only a few chat rooms and bulletin boards specifically for wedding consultants (like the chat room at www.junewedding.com, and the discussion board at www.ultimatewedding.com), there are many other sites out there where small business owners can find ideas to help them do business better. One to check out is *Entrepreneur* magazine's site at www.entrepreneur.com.

There's no charge for all the wisdom out there, beyond the cost of your internet connection. But remember: You get exactly what you pay for. Just as you can't always believe everything you see in print or on the evening news, you shouldn't necessarily believe everything you read on the internet. Everyone and anyone, from your half-baked neighbor Ernie to the president of the Rubber Band Association of America, can create a web site and post seemingly accurate information on it. So as the saying goes: *Caveat emptor*, or "Let the buyer beware." Always consider the source when searching for information, and stick with reliable and reputable people or companies. For instance, if you're looking for help with writing your business plan, you know you can trust a source like the Small Business Administration's web site, rather than one featuring "Jason's 12-Step Plan for Making Big Bucks."

As mentioned previously, the internet is also an excellent place to start your search for suppliers you can use to provide the products and services you'll need to do your job. Although not every company has its own web site, there has been a huge proliferation of new web sites in the past few years. As a result, it's likely you'll find the larger service companies, such as banquet facilities, florists, and bridal shops, out in cyberspace at your beck and call.

When you start researching vendors, you can expect their web sites to provide information like their locations, hours, and descriptions of their products or services. What you often won't find (unless the company is selling retail products) is pricing information. Generally it's omitted because companies prefer to discuss pricing with a real live person who can be persuaded to buy. But you can still accumulate enough useful data to know whether a lead is worth pursuing.

Yet another useful purpose for the internet is as a tool to fulfill the bridal party's unusual requests. Does the bride want an Elvis impersonator to serenade her like hound dog at the reception? Search on the keywords "celebrity impersonators," plus the name of your city, to see what pops up. Or maybe she remembers seeing charming replicas of 18th century tussy mussy holders in a magazine and insists on using them for her bridesmaids' bouquets. Try searching on "tussy mussy" and see where it leads you.

Important Web Addresses at a Glance

Here are some web sites you can use to do business better, find useful (free) advice, or just get a giggle:

○ *Amazon*: sells books, CDs, and videos (www.amazon.com)

○ *Dilbert*: the famous cartoon strip antihero goes interactive (www.unitedmedia/comics/dilbert)

○ *Entrepreneur*: the premier source for small-business advice (www.entrepreneur.com)

○ *e-Organizer*: a free service that e-mails reminders about important dates, chores, etc. (www.eorganizer.com)

○ *Federal Express*: an expedited delivery service (www.fedex.com)

○ *FindLaw*: for legal resources (www.findlaw.com)

○ *Google*: online search engine for information (www.google.com)

○ *Internal Revenue Service*: premier source for tax tips and advice (www.irs.gov)

○ *Mapquest*: online driving directions in the United States www.mapquest.com)

○ *National Association for the Self-Employed*: offers advice, group insurance, and more (www.nase.org)

○ *National Association of Enrolled Agents*: a source for locating accountants (www.naea.org)

○ *National Association of Home Based Businesses*: tips and information for homebased businesses (www.usahomebusiness.com)

○ *National Association of Women Business Owners*: resource, networking, and advocacy group (www.nawbo.org)

○ *National Small Business Network*: interactive resource for home-office and small-business owners (www.businessknowhow.net)

○ *Small Business Administration*: the small-business owner's best friend, with extensive FAQs and advice (www.sbaonline.sba.gov)

○ *Small Office*: a site with articles and advice for small businesses (www.smalloffice.com)

○ *Travelocity*: a site for airline and hotel reservations worldwide (www.travelocity.com)

○ *United Parcel Service*: an expedited delivery service (www.ups.com)

○ *U.S. Census Bureau*: the official government web site for statistics and demographics (www.census.gov)

○ *Wed Alert*: offers interesting and up-to-date information on weddings and wedding trends (wedalert.net)

○ *ZIP code look-up*: helps you find any zip code in the United States and its possessions (www.usps.gov)

Still another invaluable function the internet serves is as a communication medium. In addition to staying in contact with vendors concerning wedding day timetables and delivery schedules, you can keep in touch with your brides. This is especially important when you're handling arrangements for an out-of-town bride, or a career woman who's short on time.

"I often work by e-mail with my clients," says Packy B. "It's much easier to send off an e-mail than to write a letter, and it's cheaper than a phone call. I may also receive an answer back the same day. You cannot beat e-mail for efficiency."

Creating a Powerful and Persuasive Web Site

Just as you can access other companies' web sites for information about their products and services, you'll want prospective customers to find you in cyberspace, too. That means establishing your web site should be a high priority on your list of things to do as you start your business.

"A company web site is imperative!" says Robbi Ernst of June Wedding, Inc. "It is the modern brochure; as a matter of fact, the money that wedding consultants once put into designing and creating a slick, elegant, informative brochure, is equivalent to what one must put into the designing and creating of a slick, elegant, and informative web site."

This is particularly important if you live and work in a city that is a known tourist destination. It's not unusual for couples to travel to exotic places like Hawaii or cosmopolitan cities like New York for their nuptials. Disney World is another hot spot for weddings, and the resort capitalizes on this by offering its own wedding packages. So if you are willing to handle long-distance arrangements (which is easier than ever today thanks to e-mail), you need to get that web site up as soon as possible.

You don't necessarily have to be an information technology whiz or a computer programmer to get the job done. There are many do-it-yourself

> **Smart Tip** *Tip...*
>
> According to Robbi Ernst of June Wedding, Inc., these are "must have's" for your web site:
>
> - Homepage
> - "Contact Us" page
> - "About Us" page
> - Testimonials from past clients and vendors. Use names not initials after these quotes to show that these testimonials are not coming from your pen!
> - Photos (make sure you have your clients' permission to run these)
> - Your company's logo should appear on all of the pages of your web site

Entering the Blogosphere

Blogs are gaining popularity at an amazing pace. Blogs are essentially online journals or newsletters, usually with more than one author. You may find blogs useful for networking, brainstorming, and simply commiserating with other wedding consultants. These sites allow for a back-and-forth of ideas and frustrations. At times, small business owners feel somewhat isolated since they often work alone. Blogs offer you an opportunity to hook up with other wedding consultants via cyberspace. Use a search engine to find bridal blogs or check out thebridalblog.observer.com.

web page kits on the market, though you may want to consider hiring a web page developer to create one for you. Before we start the exciting process of building your cyberspace corporate identity, let's start by looking at the web site development process.

The Basics of Web Design

Because your web site is virtual advertising that's available on demand 24 hours per day, it's important to spend a fair amount of time considering what it should say. Before approaching a web site designer, consider the questions you think your customers would have when searching for a wedding consultant. Here are examples of the kinds of questions your customers might have:

- How can I set up a reasonable budget?
- What is the average amount I can expect to spend on my entire wedding?
- Can you plan my entire wedding?
- How can you help me on my wedding day?
- Can you coordinate my honeymoon arrangements?
- Can you help me find a good florist (or caterer or DJ or baker)?
- Can we correspond by e-mail, or must we meet in person?
- Is there a charge for the initial consultation?
- What do your services cost?
- How will I pay you? Do you have a payment plan?
- Do you have references?
- How can I reach you?

Armed with these questions, you should next consider how you want the site to look. You want it to be user-friendly, yet elegant so it reflects the tastes of your customers. You

Dollar Stretcher

Check out yahoositebuilder.com or web.com for inexpensive web design solutions. Starting at under $10 per month, these companies offer templates for web site design, free domain names and a web host site.

can do this by keeping the web page design clean and uncluttered, and the copy succinct. This doesn't mean you can't say what you need to say. But you don't have to tell readers every detail related to your business. You just want them to have enough information to make an informed decision about whether hiring a wedding consultant fits well with their plans—and their budgets.

Spend time looking at other wedding consultants' web sites. Keep a list of what you like and don't like about these web sites and incorporate theses findings into your design plans. For instance, color plays a powerful role in web site design. Consider carefully the hues you'll choose. Also, consider how different type faces work. You might like the idea of a swirly, script style type but remember that these type faces can be harder to read. Your number-one priority is making your web site as accessible as possible.

You'll also want to keep the copy brief because many people find it annoying to have to keep scrolling down as they read. In addition, if the text runs onto too many screens, it's harder for the customer to print material from your web page—material that you hope will induce them to call you for a consultation later.

Building Your Web Site

The next decision you must make relates to the type of web site you want to build. A simple option is the online business card, which is no more than a single screen that gives your company name and contact information, like your address, phone number, and fax number. This type of web site is actually quite easy to build, even for those who don't know a byte from a baud. There are a number of how-to internet books available in bookstores, or from online retailers like Amazon.com, that can guide you through the process of creating your own page. However, the disadvantage of this kind of web page is there's not much room for information. If you have a lot to say (and a sales pitch to make), you should consider creating an online "brochure" instead.

Online brochures are the choice of many wedding consultants precisely because they can accommodate more information. Not only can you answer the types of questions addressed above, you also can provide links (electronic connections) to your preferred vendors, your online retail store (if you plan to sell items like invitations and champagne flutes), your e-mail inquiry form, and other pertinent information. This is also a good place to discuss the details of the various packages you offer so customers have a clear idea of the scope of your services.

Portals are electronic entryways into the internet. When you access a portal like AltaVista, Excite, Yahoo!, or Google, you are tapping into a complex "web" of indices that can connect you to the sites you wish to visit. The indices are divided into categories to make surfing easier and can be accessed by typing as little as a single keyword.

Loreen C. in Ypsilanti, Michigan, relies heavily on her online brochure to promote her business. Working with a web designer, Loreen gave her site a Hollywood flair, complete with graphics, like director's clappers and studio chairs, as well as snappy copy that evokes the feeling of a professional production (she uses terms like "box office hit" and "It's showtime!").

Smart Tip

There is no quicker way to undermine your credibility than to maintain a sloppy web site. *Do not let your web site become outdated.* Nothing will turn a client off faster than finding outdated information on a web site. Also, be sure that words are not misspelled. Misspelled words reflect carelessness on your part—not what you want to convey to future clients!

She also has a lead screen with blanks the bride (or other interested surfer) can fill out and e-mail back for further information.

Home Sweet Home Page

By now you've probably realized that because your expertise lies in event planning and organization, you'll want to hire a professional web designer to create your web page. As mentioned earlier, you can design it yourself using a how-to book. But unless you're well-versed in both HTML language and graphic design, it's probably more trouble than it's worth, especially when there are professionals who are awaiting your call.

Because web designers are often also graphic designers, you can find them in the same places already discussed in Chapter 9. You should expect to work closely with your designer to make decisions about copy placement, colors, typefaces, and so on. Don't just dump the project into his or her lap. The web page should reflect your style and taste, so you should be involved in all stages of its development. But do rely on the designer's best judgment when it comes to level of interactivity, navigation tools, and artwork.

The wedding consultants we spoke to paid anywhere from $800 to $4,000 for web site design. Part of this cost is based on the number of pages on the site. The more complex the site is, the more it will cost.

Name that Domain

Like your company, your web site has to have a unique name that will be used on the server it resides on. This is called the domain name, or URL. Examples of domain names used by some of the wedding consultants we spoke to include "everafterwed dings.com," "goc.com" (an acronym for "Grand Occasions"), and "Designmywedding.com." In the bridal consulting business, using your business name as your domain name is usually your best bet, but do keep in mind that domain names must be unique, and someone else might already be using the name you've chosen. Keep in mind, too, that acronyms can be more challenging for your clients to remember.

Domain names must be registered for a minimum of two years, after which you can renew them. The cost to register a name for two years is approximately $70. There are several companies that handle registration, but the best known is DOMAIN.com, which also allows you to register your name for five- or ten-year periods. The cost for these longer registrations is $30 and $25 per year, respectively.

Your Web Host

You're now just one step away from having a live web site. That last step involves selecting the web host site where your site will reside so users can access it 24 hours a day. Examples of well-known web hosts include Microsoft Network and Prodigy, but there are many, many smaller hosts around the country. Before selecting a host, ask other business people for recommendations. You'll want to know how often the site goes down and how long it takes to fix it; whether it has reliable customer support; how many incoming lines the server has (so users don't get a busy signal when they call); whether it has experience with high traffic sites; and how big it is.

A caveat is in order here. Remember that loony neighbor we mentioned earlier? Even he can be a web host if he has the right computer equipment and telephone trunk lines installed in his dusty old attic. Unfortunately, if you take a chance with a lesser-known host you run the risk of having it go out of business or disappearing in the night, which will not inspire confidence in your customers.

As you probably expected, there is a cost for web hosting. The price of web fame starts as low as $14.95 per month. Some of the hosts will also allow you to register your domain at the same time. Web hosting is very competitive, so it pays to shop around.

The Power of the Press

In Chapter 9, we talked about the benefits of advertising your business. But, as the chapter indicated, advertising costs money—something that may be in short supply, especially when you first start your bridal business.

Fortunately, there are many low-cost marketing and public relations tools you can use to generate positive publicity

Wedding News

Afternoon remains the most popular time for taking vows, with 53 percent of all weddings taking place then. Thirty-one percent of couples opt for evening and a slim 16 percent choose the morning for the "I do's."

for your business. Among these tools are news releases, feature articles, newsletters, bridal shows, and networking. Here's a rundown of what they entail and how they can help you.

News Releases

News releases (also called press releases) are like little advertisements for your business. But they're subtler than ads, and possibly more credible to the reader because when they appear in print they look like news stories rather than advertisements. To appreciate the difference between the two, think of a 30-second TV commercial touting a popular sports drink and a longer infomercial lauding the benefits of a new exercise machine. An infomercial sounds more like a news program even though there's a sales pitch at the end. That's the same impact a well-written news release can have.

News releases differ from ads in another important way: There is no cost to run your releases in newspapers, magazines, or other print sources. But there's also no guarantee that what you write will ever appear in print. That's because editors sometimes use news releases as "idea starters" that can be developed into related or more detailed stories. They also use releases as filler material or when they have room on a page with editorial content relating to the same topic you've written about. One note: editors will also feel free to use only part of your press release. They may trim the release from five paragraphs to three paragraphs. Don't bother complaining. The editor is doing you a service by running even a portion of the news release.

Even though it's not a given that your news release will be picked up, you should still send them out faithfully and regularly. News releases are one of the most economical ways you have to promote your business, and a steady stream of releases sent to a publication will increase the chances that at least some of them will appear in print.

Tip...

Smart Tip

Newspapers won't run your press release if it sounds like an ad. That is why newspapers sell advertising space. If you are simply out to promote, don't bother approaching a newspaper. Instead, when you write your press release you must have what is known as a "hook." This hook must be something that makes your press release timely and newsworthy. Perhaps you recently held a wedding at a historic site or you've changed business locations. These are the types of hooks that will help to ensure that your press release is run.

The news outlets that are most likely to use news releases about your bridal business are newspapers, magazines, and business publications. If you have a local talk radio station or cable TV station, you might want to put those on your news release list, too.

Also, it is worthwhile to consider occasionally packaging your news release in a novel way (like sending it rolled up in a champagne flute, or securing it with a lacy garter). This presentation (and extra effort on your part) will help spark an editor's interest. Save this technique for really special news, like when you announce your business start-up, or if you've been hired to coordinate a celebrity or other important wedding.

> ## Smart Tip
> Tip...
>
> Always call to find out the name of the appropriate person to whom to send the release. Releases addressed to "Editor" or, worse yet, just the name of the publication, are far less likely to get into print. Take the extra time to find out the editor's name—these efforts will pay off in that more of your releases will make their way into print.

The first news release you'll want to write will announce the opening of your new wedding consultant business (see example on page 110). But you can write a news release about nearly anything newsworthy that relates to your business including:

- New services you're offering
- A move to a new location
- An expanded service area, such as a new focus on destination weddings
- Special discounts (i.e. discounts for weddings in the off-season)
- Addition of new staff members
- Your wedding consultant certification
- Meeting other milestones, such as planning your 100th wedding
- Special events or seasonal information (such as Valentine's Day packages)

You can also write what's known as a "backgrounder," or a news release that gives general information about your services, hours of operation, and contact information. Be sure to include biographical information about yourself (like educational background and pertinent experience) that emphasizes your qualifications. The hope is that an editor's interest will be piqued by the details about your business, and he or she will want to interview you further for a feature story. Backgrounders are a bit trickier since, as referred to earlier in this chapter, editors may feel that these releases are not "newsy" enough.

Writing the Release

A good news release will answer the five "W" questions (who, what, where, when, and why) and the "H" question (how). Put the most important information first, since

▲

Wedding Consultant News Release

NEWS RELEASE
For Immediate Release

Date: June 13, 200x
Media contact: Marie Masters
Telephone: (714) 555-0197

Wedding Consultant Makes Matrimony Into an Art Form

LOS ANGELES—Marie Masters is weeping copiously into a soggy tissue for the second time this week. But weddings always have that effect on her, so this certified wedding consultant good-naturedly sees the tears as part of her job.

"I always get a little misty-eyed when one of 'my' brides walks down the aisle," Masters says. "We work together so closely to plan her special day that I can't help being just as happy and proud as she is."

Masters is the owner and founder of *A Vision in White*, a wedding consultant business based in Chino Hills. Her task is to coordinate the seemingly insurmountable mountain of details that go into planning the perfect wedding, from securing the banquet hall to picking the menu, ordering the flowers, coordinating the newlyweds' hotel reservations, and handling everything else in between.

"And of course, the real trick is to get everything to come together correctly and on time," she says with a laugh. "Brides love turning over all those details to me."

Bridal industry statistics show that more and more women are relying on wedding consultants to coordinate the wedding of their dreams. And no wonder. Masters earns each client's trust by consulting with her every step of the way to ensure her satisfaction. She charges a flat fee for her services based on the number of tasks she's asked to coordinate. For a consultation appointment, call *A Vision in White* at (714) 555-0197.

# # #

editors tend to cut copy from the end of a release if it's too long to run in its entirety. In any event, try to keep the release short and to the point. It should be no longer than two 1.5-spaced or double-spaced pages—at the very most. If the release does flow to a second page, use the word "more" at the bottom of page one to indicate that it continues. Use three pound symbols (# # #) to indicate the end of the release.

To alert editors that what they're reading is a news release, use the format shown in the sample release on page 110. Some of the elements this format includes are:

- *Release information.* Unless your release shouldn't be published right away, it will always say "For Immediate Release" at the top.

- *Contact name.* Your name, e-mail, and phone number go here so editors can call you for further information, if needed.

- *Headline.* This is a succinct description of what the release is about. Center this line over the text of the release. Using bold type will make the headline stand out.

- *Dateline.* This is the city from which the release originates. For example, if your business is located in metropolitan Seattle, the first word before the text of the release begins should be "SEATTLE," in uppercase type.

Stat Fact

Ninety percent of news releases never get into print—often because they're incomplete, late, or full of errors. To increase the likelihood that an editor will print your release, check it carefully for typos, time it to arrive while the news is still fresh, provide interesting details that will catch his or her interest, and include a photo whenever possible. Also, don't stint on hiring help if you do not feel confident in your writing skills. You may damage your business and your credibility if you submit a poorly written news release. Freelance writers and editors are listed in your local Yellow Pages.

Impressionable Releases

Even if all of your press releases don't wend their way into print, often you are still making an impact on the editor. Robbi Ernst, of June Wedding, Inc., describes an experience about the powerful effect of sending press releases at regular intervals. "When a writer from *Modern Bride* called me to interview me for an article about wedding consultants, I asked, 'How did you come to call me?' She replied, 'Mr. Ernst, when I was assigned to write this article, I went to our files and yours is seven inches thick—full of press releases, articles, and such. I figured that you must know what you are doing, and that's the reason I called.'" In fact, this article, published in 1987, brought Ernst his first half-million dollar client!

▲

- *Text.* This is the body of the release with all the pertinent details, including the five Ws and the H.

Producing the Release

Once you've finalized your copy, you're ready to send your news release out to the companies on your mailing list. Most companies prefer—and some require—that press releases be sent via e-mail. You will send the release as an attachment. Simply note in your e-mail that you are attaching a press release for immediate release (or note the date it should be run if it is not for immediate release) and give a "thanks in advance" for the editor's efforts.

If, in fact, you come across a media outlet that prefers to receive hard copy (these will be rare since the company will then have to rely on its own staff to retype the press release information), print the release on your company letterhead using a high quality laser or ink jet printer. Standard size (8.5-by-11) white bond paper is preferred. Alternately, you can photocopy the text onto your stationery. But if your personal photocopy machine doesn't produce extremely high quality copies, consider using a quick print shop like Kinko's or American Speedy Printing, which charge a few cents per copy. If the release runs to a second page, staple the pages together. Then mail the finished releases in your company's imprinted number ten envelopes for the most professional look.

Follow-Up

Your job isn't finished once the e-mails with your press release attachment have been sent. About a week after the releases have been sent, e-mail or call each editor personally. If e-mailing, simply ask if the editor needs more information. If calling, introduce yourself, and politely inquire whether he or she has received your release and whether it's likely to be published. Be sure to ask, too, if there are specific types of information he or she is more likely to use. Make a note of these preferences so you can refer to them the next time you're drafting a release. Don't be too pushy about asking when the press release will run. Each editor is allotted a certain percentage of "news hole" or space where editorial content can run.

Feature Articles

Like news releases, feature stories are an excellent way to garner publicity for your business. What makes these articles such powerful and effective tools is the fact that they can be used to position you as an authority in your field. This is a great way to gain credibility in your field while building a solid reputation as a savvy businessperson.

Feature stories can run the gamut from informational articles to how-tos to profiles about your services. The slant you take depends on the type of publication you're planning to send them to. For instance, a story on "The Top Ten Reasons to Hire a Wedding Consultant" might be perfect for the features section of your daily newspaper. On the other hand, an article about your entrepreneurial talents, or your successful business start-up, might be more appropriate for the business section of your paper or a specialty business magazine.

Don't overlook the value of sharing your knowledge and insight with readers. The idea is to "wow" them with your creative ideas so they immediately think of you when they're ready to engage someone to coordinate their wedding celebration. So write articles giving tips for creating a beautiful wedding. Share stories about wedding disasters and how they can be averted or fixed. Or report on the spectacular wedding you coordinated for the daughter of a leading citizen in your town. People also like to read about trends, so let curious readers know what is "hot" and what is not in the world of weddings.

Although feature articles can run anywhere from 500 to 2,500 words, depending on the publication, a reasonable length is 1,000 to 1,500 words. As with news releases, you can use a freelance writer to "ghostwrite," or produce the articles under your byline. You can expect to pay a freelance ghostwriter $100 to $750 for a 1,200-word article.

Submitting Your Manuscript

Most news organizations will ask that you submit your feature article via e-mail. Send the article as an attachment. Note in your e-mail that you have attached an article about topic X. Let the editor know in a few sentences why this topic is timely and will be of interest to readers. Always remember to give information about how and where you can be reached.

Smart Tip Tip...

When submitting feature articles, pitch them to one publication at a time. By doing this, you ensure that competing weekly newspapers won't simultaneously run your article. You may like the free publicity, but the newspapers will feel hoodwinked since each newspaper may have felt your story was an exclusive. When you submit the story, ask that the editor let you know by a given date if the story will run. If you don't hear by that date, then feel free to submit your story to another news organization. Also, check with news editors before writing feature stories. Some news outlets will only print stories written solely by staff members.

Then follow up by e-mail or phone as described above to increase the chances that the article will be published.

Newsletters

If you're like most people, your mailbox is probably overflowing with newsletters from everyone from your state senator to your local nursery. There is a good reason for the proliferation of these pithy little news vehicles. They're inexpensive to produce, they are easy to create, and they're a very effective way to spread the news about any product or service you offer.

The main reason you'll want to produce a newsletter is to "upsell," or suggest other fee-generating ways you can help the bride. Say, for example, you've accepted a consulting job that consists of coordinating wedding day basics only, such as arranging for the church, setting up the reception, hiring a disk jockey, and reserving a limousine. You might be able to generate additional work—and income—by sending a newsletter with articles focusing on your honeymoon planning services, tuxedo pickup and delivery services, and so on. You could also include checklists (such as "Things to Do One Month Before the Wedding") and useful information about things like wedding software and marriage traditions.

You don't have to send a lot of newsletters to get the bride's attention. Rather, to keep the newsletter process manageable, plan on creating a single "stock" newsletter, or a generic piece that can be mailed to each new client as she engages your services. Time the delivery of the newsletter for a couple of weeks after the consultation, as a way to jog the bride's memory about the many ways you can help. Put your fee schedule and the lead time you need to complete additional projects right in the newsletter.

The newsletter itself should be written in a concise, journalistic style no matter whether the intent of its articles is to inform or solicit business. You can use one of the numerous affordable software packages available to create the newsletter yourself. It's perfectly fine to design your newsletter with all words and no artwork. Be sure to include your logo, though, if you have one. Remember that you are creating a brand and you want your logo to appear on all of your marketing materials. If you feel intimidated by the task of designing your newsletter, hire a freelance designer.

The standard size for a newsletter is 8.5 by 11 inches, and it's usually produced in multiples of four pages (although two pages—one sheet with type on the front and back—is also appropriate and easy to produce). A newsletter that's two or four pages will easily fit into a number ten envelope, which is the easiest way to mail it.

It is also appropriate to send newsletters via e-mail. This is a very inexpensive means of marketing your company. Simply make sure that your e-mail newsletter is finding willing recipients. No one likes finding unsolicited mail in their computer's in

Dollar Stretcher

Printing your newsletter in no more than two colors will help keep costs down. If you have a very high quality laser printer and just a small quantity of newsletters to print, you might consider printing them yourself. But remember that printing takes valuable time, and unless the newsletter is printed on a high quality paper stock, it might look chintzy. Generally, you should opt for professional printing (or at least Speedy Printing) instead.

box. In other words, don't spam clients. Check first to make sure they would like to be on your newsletter e-mail list.

Consider including a special offer in the newsletter—perhaps a discount on the initial consultation. This will help you to track how many people are reading and using your newsletter.

Bridal Shows

For sheer numbers, there may be no better place to gain quick exposure for your business than a bridal show. These events attract hundreds, or even thousands, of brides-to-be—women who will definitely be consumers of the services you offer.

Bridal shows are generally held in convention centers in large cities. For a fairly reasonable price (anywhere from $600 to $1,300, on average), you can rent booth space in these shows. Then it's up to you to chat up prospective customers, cheerfully hand out your business card and brochure, and otherwise lay the groundwork that will result in new business.

Although it's possible to make a professional impression using just the 10- or 12-foot skirted table that's usually provided with your space, you can also personalize your display area. Since you'll be competing with other companies that offer the same kinds of products and services, strive to be innovative. Use a dressmaker's mannequin to display a lovely vintage wedding gown. Artfully display large photographs of weddings you've coordinated on lace-festooned easels. Or invest in a pre-fab booth that can be set up quickly right in your space.

These ten-foot high booths have a steel skeleton that's covered with fabric panels that can support signage, photographs, and other visuals. This kind of display is set up at the back of your booth as a backdrop. There's a wide variety of styles to choose from including single-unit panels with custom designs, or triple-units. The multi-unit displays usually require lighting to give them pizzazz.

These booths are easy to assemble and tear down. But while such booths are very eye-catching, they can run from $800 and up for the single panel model up into the stratosphere. They also don't usually include the graphics, which you'll have to have created separately by a graphic designer. The halogen lights recommended for these displays run about $139 each.

A more cost effective way to exhibit is by using a tabletop display. As the name implies, it sits right on the table, leaving you space to display brochures or other handout materials. These displays come in several configurations and run about $1,100, excluding the cost of the graphics.

This probably sounds pretty pricey, especially for a start-up operation. But if you're planning to attend many bridal shows, the investment is worth it in terms of the professional image you'll project.

Another way to attract show attendees to your booth is by holding a drawing for a wedding-themed gift. For instance, you might invite visitors to fill out an entry form for a chance to win a pair of champagne flutes or a floral arrangement for the rehearsal dinner. One lucky winner will take home a gift (or a promissory note in the case of flowers), and you'll take home a bowl-full of entry forms with the names and addresses of prospective clients. These prospects should immediately go on your mailing list so you can send them a newsletter you've developed especially for this purpose.

Weigh the costs carefully before committing to a bridal show. Many consultants simply don't find the payoff big enough to attend these events.

"For brides attending bridal shows, the last thing on their minds and on their to-do list is choosing a wedding consultant," says Ann Nola, of the Association of Certified Professional Wedding Consultants.

Packy B., the Ohio wedding consultant, says she has found that bridal shows aren't always the best possible venue for attracting new business, but they still serve an important purpose. "Bridal shows give you visibility with the public, even if they don't generate a lot of business," she says. "They also give you a chance to meet and network with a lot of vendors all in one place."

Tip...

Smart Tip

Don't just exchange pleasantries and business cards when you network at professional business organization meetings. Plan a follow-up meeting with people whose interests mesh with yours, or those who might even be potential clients. Just be sure to make a notation on the back of their cards so you'll remember why you're pursuing the relationship.

Bright Idea

Some wedding consultants package all their promotional and sales materials in a media kit, which can be given out to business prospects. Some of the items in the kit (usually organized in a pocket folder) may include a letter thanking the client for his or her interest, a "backgrounder" and other news releases, a brochure, and the owner's biography and photograph. Remember to include your logo on this kit, perhaps on the front of the pocket folder. You want your clients to connect your logo with your business.

Julia K., the wedding consultant in Oak Point, Texas, concurs. She says, "Bridal shows are great—and I mean really great—for building credibility among vendors. We set up our booth an hour or two early before the other vendors, then go around and offer snacks and assistance to those who are scrambling to finish in time. They would get a chance to see firsthand how we can make their lives easier the day of the wedding and would begin recommending us without actually having worked with us at a wedding before."

Networking

You know the old saying: "It's not what you know, but who you know." Well, it holds true in the wedding business, as well. The more people you know in this field, the easier it will be to locate and land new business.

Two extremely valuable networking sources are your local chamber of commerce and Rotary Club. These organizations consist of both small- and large-business owners, and encourage their members to exchange ideas, support each other's businesses, and barter services. The cost to join either organization is reasonable, and you can quickly build a reputation as a caring and reputable business owner by becoming involved in the groups' public service activities.

You might also consider joining other professional business organizations in your area, such as economic clubs or women business owners' groups. Then get involved in the leadership of the group. That way, your name will be top of mind when one of the members is looking for or knows someone who needs a wedding consultant.

Finally, professional wedding consultant organizations are a good place to meet other planners and share tips and techniques. Many of the national organizations have regional chapters that hold regular meetings. See the Appendix for contact information.

12

Keeping Track
of Your Finances

By now, you should be pretty jazzed about becoming a wedding consultant and feel like you're ready to take on the world. But there's one itty bitty little thing you still have to work on because it can mean the difference between startling success and abysmal failure. We're talking, of course, about financial management.

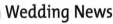

Alas, this is the point where many people turn pale and cast their eyes skyward in supplication. But maybe you're one of the lucky ones. Maybe you excelled in math and accounting in school, so you're not phased by the thought of balance sheets and cash-flow statements. Or maybe you earned a bachelor's degree in business administration in a previous life and find the real challenge in this job to be soothing weepy brides or dealing with prima donna vendors.

But if you're like many wedding consultants, who are long on enthusiasm, creativity, and common sense and perhaps a wee bit short on financial acumen, don't despair. Help is available. You just have to know where to look for it.

Key Financial Statements

Keeping good records helps generate the financial statements that tell you exactly where you stand and what you need to do next. These statements are vital in developing the growth—and problem areas—of your developing wedding consultant business.

The key financial statements you need to understand and use regularly are:

- *Profit and loss statement* (also called the P&L or the income statement). This statement illustrates how much your company is making or losing over a designated period—monthly, quarterly, or annually—by subtracting expenses from your revenue to arrive at a net result, which is either a profit or a loss.

- *Balance sheet.* A balance sheet is a table showing your assets, liabilities, and capital at a specific point. A balance sheet is typically generated monthly, quarterly, or annually when the books are closed.

- *Cash flow statement.* This summarizes the operating, investing, and financing activities of your business as they relate to the inflow and outflow of cash. As with the profit and loss statement, a cash flow statement is prepared to reflect a specific accounting period, such as monthly, quarterly, or annually.

Be sure to review these statements at a regular interval, at least monthly. In this way you can quickly move to correct minor difficulties before they become major financial problems.

A professional accountant can help you generate these statements or you can check out intuit.com for a variety of software applications that will be useful to your wedding consultant business. From tax preparation to financial management applications specifically designed for small companies, these products will help you streamline your financial management.

A sample of a profit and loss worksheet appears on page 123, showing how this simple form will help you to estimate your operating costs and project your earnings. The statement on page 122 shows the operating costs for our two hypothetical wedding consulting businesses: one that's homebased, and another that operates out of a small commercial space. While not all of the expenses we'll discuss will apply to you, here's a rundown of the typical expenses a homebased wedding consultant can expect to incur.

Smart Tip *Tip...*

It is always a good idea to keep separate accounts, one for personal use and one for your wedding consultant business expenses. Use a separate checking account as well as separate credit cards for all of your business expenditures. This will help to ensure accurate record keeping and prove extremely helpful when tax season arrives.

Telephone Calls

If you have a business telephone line, you should note the total cost of the bill, including both zone and long-distance calls. Your cellular phone bill should be included in this amount if the phone is used strictly for business. You should plan on having a phone line dedicated solely to your business. Some consultants choose their cell phone as their business number.

If you're still using your home phone as your business line, estimate only the cost of the zone and long-distance calls made for business, since Uncle Sam won't allow you to deduct the entire phone bill on your business tax return. A word of advice: Keep a handwritten log of telephone calls that you can compare against your phone bill every month. The IRS usually requires written records for any expenses you deduct, and it will be much easier to figure which calls are legitimate business expenses if you have a log to refer to. It may be easier to have a phone dedicated solely to your business since keeping this log can be time consuming and onerous.

Telephone charges are likely to make up the lion's share of the service fees you'll pay on a monthly basis. Thanks to the deregulation of the phone company a number of years ago, these charges vary regionally, but it's reasonable to estimate a cost of $25 per line. Useful features you'll want to consider adding to your basic service include voice mail ($6 to $20 per month), call waiting (approximately $5 per month), and caller ID (around $7.50 for number identification, and an additional $2 for name and number identification).

Your cellular phone is billed at a totally different rate. There are many great usage deals around right now, ranging from $4.99 a month for a no-minute basic package

Sample Profit/Loss

Here are sample income/operating expenses statements for our two hypo-thetical wedding consulting businesses that reflect typical operating costs for this industry. "Weddings by Jamie" is the homebased business that averages 12 weddings per year. "Cherished Moments in Time" handles 20 to 30 wed-dings per year and operates out of a small space in a commercial building. You can compute your own projected income and expenses using the work-sheet on page 123.

	Weddings by Jamie	Cherished Moments
Projected Monthly Income	$1,000	$3,000
Projected Monthly Expenses		
Rent	$0	$500
Phone (office and cellular)	$40	$65
Utilities	$0	$50
Postage	$50	$50
Employee payroll/benefits	$0	$200
Advertising	$60	$125
Maintenance	$0	$50
Accounting services	$0	$100
Transportation	$0	$50
Loan repayment	$0	$125
Online service	$20	$20
Web site hosting	$20	$20
Miscellaneous expenses (stationery and other office supplies)	$25	$50
Total Expenses	(−$215)	(−$1,405)
Projected Monthly Net Income	$785	$1,595

Profit/Loss Worksheet

Projected Monthly Income $ _____

Projected Monthly Expenses $ _____

Rent $ _____

Phone (office and cellular) $ _____

Utilities $ _____

Postage $ _____

Employee payroll/benefits $ _____

Advertising $ _____

Insurance $ _____

Maintenance $ _____

Accounting services $ _____

Stationery and office supplies $ _____

Transportation $ _____

Loan repayment $ _____

Online service $ _____

Web hosting $ _____

Total Expenses (−$——————)

Projected Monthly Net Income $ _____

> **Beware!**
> Don't stint on your cell phone minutes when you choose a plan. Cell phone providers really sock it to their customers when they use more than their allotted minutes. Don't get caught short; buy a plan with ample time.

(minutes are charged separately at a rate of 25 to 45 cents each), to $39.99 for 600 minutes or more. Because these high-end packages are so reasonable, you might want to opt for one right off the bat, since you'll be locked into a certain rate plan for a predetermined number of years anyway. What's really great is that many of these package plans offer thousands of minutes of calling time free on the weekend—which will probably be your peak calling time. You can also expect to pay an activation fee of around $30 if you don't sign up for a three-year contract.

Pagers are another option and are probably the best value around for keeping in touch. Many rate plans cost $60 or less for a full year of service that's billed upfront, either annually or quarterly.

Office Supplies

This includes all the paper clips, stationery, business cards, and other supplies you need to do business every day. Obviously, some expenses like business printing won't be incurred every month, so use the figure you found when you priced your stationery and business cards, and divide by 12. This number is added to the other costs you estimate for the month.

Postage

You will be mailing contracts to clients, confirmation letters to vendors, and possibly direct mail pieces to prospective clients. If you anticipate having monthly shipping charges, include those, too.

You may choose to rent a post-office box, or a box at a mailing center like Mail Boxes Etc., as a way of keeping your business mail separate from your personal mail. This service fee will run around $10 to $20 per month.

Wages

This is what you'll pay the contract or temporary employees who will help you with on-site wedding day management, clerical tasks in the office, and so on. Many wedding consultants pay their helpers $10 to $15 per hour, while some pay a minimum of $100 for a daylong event. Try hiring college students or young adults right out of high school (any younger and you'll have to worry about them trying to make the altar boys laugh during the blessing of the rings, or staging an impromptu toga party using the Battenberg lace table linens). Young adults are usually ecstatic to accept even the low-end wage, since jobs in fast food or retailing pay much less.

In general, it's best to do your own hiring rather than using an employment agency to provide temporary or leased employees. Agencies tack a hefty service fee (as much as 40 percent) onto the basic hourly rate you'll pay, which can quickly erode your profits. Instead, try placing a brief want ad in your local community newspaper. Since most people love weddings, you should get a respectable number of responses, which will give you a nice pool of applicants to choose from.

Also, don't overlook stay-at-home moms or retirees as prospective employees. Retirees in particular make wonderful employees—they're usually very happy to help out however they can. Just make sure they have the stamina to be on their feet for long periods of time. By the same token, make sure any moms you hire have a reliable babysitter so you're not left to juggle the demands of a nervous bride and 500 hungry guests all by yourself some Saturday night.

Fortunately, unless you hire full-time employees, you aren't required to pay any benefits or withhold federal taxes or FICA from workers' paychecks. The contractors themselves are responsible for ponying up with the Feds. However, the IRS requires you to file Form 1099-MISC for every contractor whose annual wages exceed $600.

Local colleges and universities are often a wonderful source for finding part-time employees. Check their web sites or post your business needs and job opportunities on campus bulletin boards.

Community newspapers are also an excellent tool for unearthing prospective employees. Not only are their classified rates quite reasonable; they're also read by people who live right in the area where you do business. Their familiarity with your market area is a plus, and their proximity to your work site increases the chances they'll always be on time.

Insurance

In addition to the rider on your existing homeowner's insurance policy, or your business owner's insurance policy, you should include the cost to insure the primary vehicle you'll use to travel to weddings and business appointments. As with the phone expenses, you should only note business-specific expenses. So if you use your vehicle to transport the kids to soccer or to go shopping, you'll have to estimate what percentage of the car is actually used for your business, then apply that to your insurance cost to arrive at a useable number. One reliable way to do this that the IRS will find acceptable is to keep a simple mileage log. Office supply stores sell mileage logbooks that are small enough to stash in your glove compartment or a pocket of your visor.

▲

Transportation

You're allowed to deduct mileage on your business tax return each year, but in the meantime, you have to spring for gas money, windshield wiper fluid, and other travel-related costs. If you work in a metropolitan area like New York, you will also have public transportation costs that can be penciled in on your profit/loss statement.

Online Service Fees

This one is easy to predict since you will sign up for service at a set price when you sign on for the first time. You will incur a monthly charge billed in advance to your credit card to connect your computer to the internet. You normally have four service choices. The least expensive service is delivered by an internet service provider (ISP), which charges $20 to $25 per month for unlimited usage and uses the modem that comes with your computer. For faster connection and transmission of data, you can choose an ISDN (Integrated Services Digital Network) line. This connection requires a setup fee of $200, a terminal or modem that costs $250, and a monthly fee of around $50.

For faster service yet, you can choose a DSL (Digital Subscriber Line). The setup fee for a DSL line is $100, while the terminal or modem will cost $250. Your monthly fee will be $40 to $60 for basic service.

Finally, cable modem service is available. It requires a setup fee of $100, a modem priced at $200 to $300, and a monthly fee of $50.

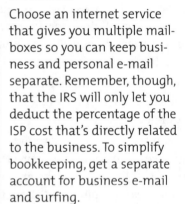

Dollar Stretcher

Choose an internet service that gives you multiple mailboxes so you can keep business and personal e-mail separate. Remember, though, that the IRS will only let you deduct the percentage of the ISP cost that's directly related to the business. To simplify bookkeeping, get a separate account for business e-mail and surfing.

Other Miscellaneous Expenses

Don't forget to add up the cost of your dry cleaning (you have an image to uphold!) and the cost of any food, snacks, or incidentals (like hairspray, panty hose, etc.) that you provide to the bridal party.

Receivables

At last, here's the good part! If all is right with the world, the money you receive from your clients will offset all the operating expenses you just read about. Hopefully, you'll have a little change to jingle in your pocket after paying all the bills. But the only way you'll know where you stand is if you keep careful records of your receivables.

You can either design your own sheet for receivables or customize a standard accountant's columnar pad available at any office supply store. These pads come with two to 12 or more columns to keep your accounting tidy. Usually, a six-column pad will do the job nicely. It's low-tech, but it works for people who are not computer-literate. If you decide to invest in an accounting software package (discussed in further detail below), you can log your receivables right on your computer and always have a running total available.

Billing Your Clients

Of course, to obtain all that lovely remuneration, you have to bill your clients regularly. You'll find a sample invoice you can adapt to your specifications on page 128. Most of the wedding consultants we spoke to bill incrementally. Typically, they require payment for the consultation on the spot, then expect monthly payments for weddings that are planned over a very long period of time (like nine months to a year). Weddings that have a shorter lead time may be billed in two installments: one at the time of the contract, and a second final payment 30 days after the event. Some consultants actually require full payment before the big day since couples can be financially strapped after the wedding and unable to pay.

Cancellations are not uncommon in this business, and Loreen C., the consultant in Michigan, tries to keep hers to a minimum by refunding just half of the deposit if the cancellation occurs within seven days. After that, the deposit is forfeited. "I have to do that because I might have turned someone else down for the same date," she explains.

Some of the wedding consultants we spoke to have merchant accounts, which allow them to bill their clients' credit cards. Julia K. points out that credit card fees can be very high for the merchant (that's you), but they're a necessary expense if you wish to be paid on a timely basis. But if you haven't been in business very long, a merchant account probably isn't necessary just yet.

> ### Tip...
>
> ### Smart Tip
> Always provide a written contract that spells out your responsibilities and payment terms, since under the Uniform Commercial Code, contracts for the sale of services or goods in excess of $500 must be in writing to be legally enforceable. Even if your bill will be under $500, it's a good idea to have a written contract just in case a dispute arises.

High-Tech Bookkeeping

Remember that financial help we talked about at the start of this chapter? It's available

Invoice for Wedding Consultant Business

Cherished
Moments

25771 Waterloo Drive
Lake Buena Vista, Florida 00003

June 23, 200x   Terms: Net 30

Sold To:

Susan Pfeiffer
49855 Petrucci Drive
Clinton Township, FL 00003

Full service "Wedding Extravaganza" consulting/coordination package $3,000

Pfeiffer/Roberts Nuptials

June 13, 200x

TOTAL   **$3,000**

Thank You!

in the form of affordable user-friendly accounting and business software you can buy at nearly any office supply or computer store. The hands-down choice of the wedding professionals we interviewed was QuickBooks by Intuit. The 2007 Pro version allows you to create invoices, track receivables, write checks and pay bills, and more. It also interfaces with Microsoft Word, Excel, and other software. Another plus: Data from QuickBooks can also be imported directly into income tax preparation packages like Turbo Tax, if you're brave enough to do your own business or personal taxes (not recommended if your tax situation is complex).

One of the best reasons to use accounting software is to prevent inadvertent math errors. All you have to do is put in the right numbers, and, voilà, they're crunched correctly.

Where the Money Is

Now you have all your ducks in a row, and they're ready to quack. Your business plan is exemplary, and you have solid evidence that your community or metropolitan area has the well-heeled economic base necessary to support your fledgling business. So financing should be a snap, right?

In your dreams. Small-business owners sometimes find it's pretty hard to find a bank willing to work with them. This is usually because the mega rich banks are far more interested in funding large companies that need large amounts of capital. They're also leery about dealing with one-person and start-up companies that don't have a long track record of success. So you may have trouble finding banking services like financing and merchant accounts that meet your small business needs.

One way around this problem is to shop around to find the bank that will welcome the opportunity to work with you. "Small business owners usually do better by selecting a bank with a community banking philosophy," says Robert Sisson, vice president and commercial business manager of Citizens Bank in Sturgis, Michigan, and author of *Show Me the Money* (Adams Media Corp.). "These are the banks that support their communities and function almost as much as a consultant as a bank."

You probably already have a pretty good idea who the smaller banking players are in your community. Start by checking out their annual reports (which you can usually find at branch offices) for clues about their financial focus and business outlook. Important clue: Institutions that support minority- and women-owned businesses as well as small businesses are likely to be more willing to help your business. Next, look for information about the number of loans they make to small companies. That's a pretty good indicator of their community commitment. Finally, study their overall business mix and the industries they serve.

While it's not impossible to find a big bank that will welcome you into the financial fold, it's actually far more likely that a warm welcome will come from a smaller financial institution.

"Small banks traditionally are better for small businesses because they're always looking for ways to accommodate these customers," says Wendy Thomas, senior business consultant at the Michigan Small Business Development Center (SBDC) at the One Stop Capital Shop

Stat Fact
According to the Small Business Development Center, all banks use certain key factors to determine a business' credit worthiness. These criteria include: collateral (assets to secure the loan), capital (owner's equity), conditions (anything that affects the financial climate), character (personal credit history), and cash flow (ability to support debts, expenses).

▲

Self-Financing Made Easy

Financing your wedding consulting start-up with your personal credit cards can save you both the hassle of applying for a bank loan and the hefty costs that can be associated with it. Of course, the downside is that you'll probably pay interest rates of as much as 24.9 percent. So if you decide to use plastic, use a card with the lowest interest rate. Call around for rates; credit card providers often will sometimes offer lower rates when you call and negotiate with them.

If your credit is good, you may be able to obtain a separate small-business line of credit through your credit card company. This allows you to borrow as much as $25,000, with no cost other than an application fee, and at a rate that's probably a lot less than what your bank would charge for a similar line of credit. American Express is one company that offers such a small-business line of credit.

Tapping into the equity in your home is another good way to secure funding. Banks now offer up to 125 percent equity loans. Just remember that your house is the collateral for the loan, and if the business doesn't do well and you can't make the payments, you could lose your home.

If you choose to finance your business through credit, proceed with extreme caution. Interest on these lines of credit can quite quickly eat up any profit you might make.

in Detroit. "Small banks are simply more willing to deal with small business concerns and are more sensitive to issues like the need for longer accounts receivable periods."

Your carefully crafted business plan will be an important tool when you approach a bank for financing. This plan shows the bank that you have thoroughly researched your business and that you have a feasible and reasonable plan for success.

Government Financing

Even if you do find a bank friendly to small businesses, you may still have trouble establishing credit or borrowing money as a start-up business. Banks, both large and small, are always more reluctant to part with their cash when the business owner doesn't have a proven track record of success.

That's where agencies like the Small Business Administration (SBA) can help. The SBA offers tons of free services to small business owners, including counseling and training seminars on topics like business plan or marketing plan development. The idea is to help the owner understand what the bank will want from him or her before ever setting foot inside the front door, thus improving the chances of being approved for a loan or other financial services.

The SBA also offers a number of different loan programs, counseling, and training. For more information, check the SBA's web site at www.sba.gov, or call the answer desk at (800) 8-ASK-SBA.

Do-It-Yourself Financing

Even with all the financing options out there, some newly established wedding consultants prefer to whip out their plastic to buy office equipment, pens, staplers, and the other goodies that make the business go. Others rely on loans from friends and family. But no matter what you do, make sure the process is handled in a professional, businesslike way. If you borrow from loved ones, sign a promissory note that details repayment terms and an equitable interest rate. Nothing can break up a tight knit family faster than a broken promise of repayment, or a misunderstanding of how the repayment will be handled. Your new business is important, but your family is precious. Protect it just like you would protect your business assets.

If you use your personal credit cards, watch your expenses closely. You can easily put yourself thousands of dollars in debt if you are not careful. Start out with the bare minimum whenever possible so your business will have a chance to grow and prosper without the specter of debt hanging over it.

As outlined in Chapter 6, launching your wedding consultant business does not necessarily mean incurring great cost. For instance, use the family computer you already own. Don't rush out to buy a new computer equipped with fancy bells and whistles until your company starts to generate a profit. Or, forgo costlier printed newsletters and, instead, rely on e-mail to distribute your news. Use what you already own to keep start-up costs low.

Learning from Your Experience

In Chapter 1, we mentioned how wedding consultants make dreams come true for happy couples. We know you have your own dream: the dream of owning a successful business that allows you to do something you love. It is our hope that all your plans and hard work pay off, and you enjoy both happiness and longevity in your newly chosen career. But

Wedding News

One-third of those getting married have been married before. The median age for remarriage is 34 for women and 37 for men.

while we wish you the best as you embark on this exciting new venture, we must acknowledge that every new business owner faces pitfalls that could threaten his or her company.

According to the National Federation of Independent Business (NFIB), 39 percent of small businesses are profitable, 30 percent break even, 30 percent lose money and 1 percent can't be determined.

The U.S. Census Bureau reports that 99.9 percent of business closures occur among small companies. In fact, many small businesses don't make it through the very first year. While this may sound discouraging, NFIB research shows that many small businesses close, not because of financial problems, but rather from a lack of interest in pursuing the business any longer. So, the high failure rate is a bit misleading in that some small-business owners simply choose to shutter their businesses—even if profitable. However, it is true that small businesses remain vulnerable. That is why careful planning is so critical to your success.

Help to Ensure Your Success

Surveys by organizations like the Small Business Administration have shown that the reasons for these failures are numerous. Business failures can be due to market conditions (such as competition or increases in the cost of doing business), financing and cash flow problems, poor planning, mismanagement, and a host of other problems. Wedding consultants in particular are susceptible to additional difficulties fostered by poor communication, bad vendor relations, personal or family illnesses, and under-priced services.

Smart Tip

Tip...

The SBA reports that too many small business owners in financial straits don't call for help until it's too late to salvage their company. Don't fall into this trap. If you ever need help, call the SBA, which can provide advice and direction, or act as a loan guarantor. There's no charge for this service, and it could save everything you've worked so hard for.

This is why we strongly recommend that you hire professionals like attorneys, bookkeepers, accountants, and contract employees to assist you in the proper management and operation of your business. Because no matter how enthusiastic, knowledgeable, and bright you may be, you're probably not an expert in every field, and your time will only stretch so far. In the beginning, it can be pretty hard to part with the cash to pay those professional fees, but in the long run, it's worth it because this kind of help will allow you to focus your attention on the things you do best.

And by the way, the outlook for success in a new business isn't completely bleak. Statistics suggest that the longer you're in business, the better your chances of staying afloat. Dun & Bradstreet reports that 70 percent of small businesses are still in business eight and a half years later. That's not a bad outlook considering the capricious nature of both consumers and the economy.

Hindsight Is 20/20

Now that your wedding consultant business is up and running, it is time to review your progress so far. As with all aspects of life, there are certainly things you might do differently now that you have some experience under your wedding garter!

Nearly every wedding consultant interviewed for this book readily admitted there were things he or she would do differently if it were possible to start again. For instance, Julia K., the wedding consultant in Oak Point, Texas, says she would have selected a partner who was more committed.

"Specifically, I ran the daytime activities, and she ran the evening activities because she chose not to give up her daytime job," Julia says. "That meant she was working way too many hours in total, and I felt compelled to take more and more of her work so that she could have some downtime every week. If I did it over, I would insist that both my partner and I were equally committed to doing only the wedding consulting so neither of us was too overworked."

Paula L., a wedding consultant in San Clemente, California, thinks she started out meeting the vendors in the industry too slowly, and if she had to start over, would speed up that process since that's the way to get a handle on the industry.

Lisa M., in Bozeman, Montana, would have advertised more, something she didn't do much of in the early days because of the constraints of her initial budget. She also would have revamped her prices sooner, something she did (with much success) after she realized

Smart Tip

Tip...

Make time to meet with other wedding consultants and others in the wedding business to share ideas and tips and to brainstorm. Perhaps, you could arrange a standing monthly morning coffee for these meetings. Just as you network to find the best vendors, it is critical to learn from other consultants the top tips for making the big day perfect—and you will have an opportunity to share your advice as well. This is also an opportunity to vent and let off steam about any frustrations you might be feeling as you develop your business.

that people who came for the free introductory meeting didn't book her because her prices didn't fit the area she serves.

But even though every wedding consultant can identify something he or she could have done better, in every case these intrepid entrepreneurs used creative thinking, hard work, and good old-fashioned determination to meet whatever challenges faced them. Obviously, this is a strategy that works. These consultants survived that scary first year, and some of them have been prospering for decades.

Was it a miracle they persevered in the face of economic uncertainties and other pressures? Definitely not. It's due more to having the right stuff and knowing how to use it. It's also due to being willing to go the extra mile, which often results in acquiring a reputation as a miracle worker when it comes to solving the crises that can crop up in the course of planning and executing a dream wedding fit for a princess.

Wedding Stories to Learn From

Being able to think fast and execute plans on the spot can mean the difference between an ecstatic bride and one who is inconsolable. As wedding consultant Lisa K. puts it, "A good wedding consultant has to be prepared for any zinger that comes her way and she has to be able to wear many, many hats."

"She Was Out $150,000"

For one New York City bride-to-be, her biggest mistake was choosing not to hire a wedding consultant.

Deborah McCoy, President of American Academy of Wedding Professionals™, remembers this bride and her mother.

"When I opened my bridal salon, a bride-to-be and her mother purchased their gowns from me. The bride was a New York City lawyer and her mom, who had planned innumerable parties, thought that planning her daughter's wedding would be a cinch. Unfortunately, a few months before the wedding, the mother called to say that her daughter cancelled the wedding and she was out $150,000 in deposits.

"If she had hired a wedding consultant she would not have lost the money. I would have negotiated the contract to include statements that would have protected her. Contracts should protect *both* the vendor and the person hiring the vendor."

In her work as a consultant, McCoy has protected many clients by creating iron-clad contracts which protect the brides- and grooms-to-be from this sort of financial debacle.

Saving the Day

Julia K. earned her wings as a wedding day angel when she came to the rescue of a bride whose bower of flowers didn't materialize. The bride, who hired Julia to coordinate a wedding for 500 guests, insisted on using a florist friend to do the flowers. Because the bride was a liquor distributor, she bartered with the florist to provide $300 worth of liquor in exchange for the wedding day flowers. All of this was done without the benefit of a contract.

Two weeks before the wedding, Julia learned that the florist had gone out of business and someone else had taken over the business. Of course, the new owner knew nothing about the floral order. So even though she wasn't officially in charge of the floral arrangements, Julia sprang into action and persuaded the new owner to design the bouquets and reception arrangements without charge, using flowers, glassware, and floral containers donated by two of her regular florist suppliers. Julia donated candles from her own stock, so the caterer could create decorations for the tables using donated rose bowls and hurricane lamps. All of the product was delivered right to the reception site, and everything was completed in time for the reception.

"The amazing thing about all this was the original florist showed up before the wedding with a bucket of cheap leatherleaf greenery and started putting it into our arrangements," Julia says. "We yanked it all out after he left."

Julia credits her relationship with her vendors, her staff, and her own experience for being able to pull off such a feat on such short notice. She believes that if the client would have tried to solve this problem herself, the story probably wouldn't have had the happy ending it had for all concerned—even Julia herself, who says, "This woman has sent us more referrals than anyone else I've worked with."

The Case of the Disappearing Guests

It's not unusual for summer showers or winter flurries to put a damper on a carefully planned wedding. But Lisa M. had to fight the forces of nature to pull off the nuptials on one memorable summer day.

Lisa was engaged to coordinate wedding day activities for a ceremony that was scheduled to take place on U.S. Forest Service land. Unfortunately, three days before the wedding, the Forest Service closed all the parks in the state of Montana because of the extreme threat of fire danger. The bride managed to locate an alternate site on private land about five miles up the road, but there wasn't enough parking to accommodate all the guests. So Lisa had to make arrangements to bus the guests to the new site instead.

"Apparently there was some confusion about where the new place was because, at 5:15 P.M., we still had no guests for the 5:30 P.M. ceremony!" Lisa says. "I had brought

Flutter Bye?

Although some brides and grooms are choosing to release butterflies as they exit the church or synagogue, try to discourage this idea. According to the North American Butterfly Association, releasing butterflies outside of their native habitat can be extremely detrimental to both the butterflies and the environment. Releasing butterflies at a wedding's close can cause genetic problems within the butterfly population. Also, if the butterflies are released in a climate that is not conducive to their well being, they could immediately die. Finally, it is critical that scientists be able to track butterflies' immigration patterns. Artificial releases undermine their efforts to do so. Try throwing serpentines, instead. These colorful spirals can be easily swept up and cause no damage—to the happy couple or to the environment.

my husband along to assist me that day, so I sent him up the road to look for the bus. The driver had gone about a mile past the turn and was starting to wonder where he had gone wrong. The guests were so happy to be rescued, they started applauding. I was glad I was there to worry about the guests so the bride and the mother-of-the-bride could enjoy the day."

Head Over Heels

Loreen C., the Michigan wedding consultant, always takes a tool kit with personal supplies for the bride, and a utility kit full of tools for herself to every wedding she coordinates. But one of the things she didn't used to pack was super bonding glue. That is, until a mishap with a cake brought the omission to her attention.

"While we were setting up for a reception, the DJ hit the cake table with a cord," Loreen says. "The cake topper fell off the cake, and the groom's head came right off. I bring a lot of extra things with me, but I never have a back-up cake topper. I also didn't have any super glue."

But the quick-thinking wedding consultant did have nail glue in her purse, so while her assistant smoothed out the frosting on the top layer of the cake, Loreen reattached the groom's little head and no one was the wiser. "I sure never said a word about it!" she says.

Speaking of coming to the rescue, that's the idea behind the tool kits Loreen brings along on wedding days. Some of the things in her tool kit (besides super glue) are a hammer, nails, screwdriver, tape, tape measure, decorator straight pins (for tasks like attaching lights to tablecloths or pinning ivy), wire cutters, extension cord, glue gun, rope (presumably not to use on a reluctant groom), and office supplies. The bride's customized kit contains things of a more personal nature, such as Tylenol, antacid, ginger ale, panty hose, mints, face powder, body lotion, lip gloss, makeup, perfume, hairspray, and a small water cup.

"I have each bride fill out a little survey in advance so I know her preferences and sizes when I put her kit together," Loreen says.

Ants for the Memory

Julia K. had her own close encounter with a wedding cake when she was supervising a rehearsal at an old mansion, while a reception for a different wedding was being set up in another room. "I happened to look into the empty room, when I passed by and noticed the cake," Julia says. "From a distance, it looked like parts of it were moving, so I went in for a closer look and saw it was covered with thousands of ants."

Neither the caterer nor—luckily—the bride were anywhere in sight. So even though she was not coordinating that particular wedding, Julia calmly removed the top layer of the cake, which mercifully was untouched by the bugs, sprayed the rest of the layers with bug spray, and blew off the dead insects. She then made arrangements with a local grocery store to provide sheet cakes free of charge that could be served instead of the ruined cake.

"In the South, the cake is usually cut in front of the guests, but this time it was wheeled into the kitchen so no one ever knew a thing," Julia says. "This kind of problem with insects actually is more common in the South than you might think because of the heat and humidity. I just insisted the facility spray for bugs the next day so I didn't have problems, too."

Your Formula for Success

It's easy to see that the kind of flexibility exhibited by Deborah McCoy and the other consultants mentioned here is one of the hallmarks of being a professional in this field. "You can't be a dramatic person in this business," Julia stresses. "You also can't let the bride see that you're upset. You have to smile when you're upset, or when you're dressing down a vendor, or when you're worried because a car hit a utility pole and knocked out the power two hours before the reception. You have to be fast on your feet and even faster than the bride."

You also have to be very committed to making your business a success. "We don't go on vacation," says Jenny C., a wedding consultant in Texas. "Everyday is an adven-

Signs of Success

You now know about the red flags that can signal a business failure. So what are the signs that your wedding consulting business will be successful?

1. You are providing a useful service at a price the market can bear.
2. Your local business market has enough customers to support your business.
3. You have enough savings or financing to weather the three-year make-or-break period.
4. Your business and marketing plans are sound, and you know where to go if you need help implementing them.
5. You have a good team of support service providers.
6. Your top priority is providing great customer service to your brides.
7. You keep careful records and always know where your business stands financially.
8. You're always aware of what your competition is up to.
9. You're flexible enough to change your business strategy when the situation warrants it.
10. You truly love your job and can't imagine doing anything else!

ture as it is."

Organization and mediation skills rank high on Loreen's personal list of required skills. "A lot of times you have to step in and keep the peace because the family wants something one way, while the bride and groom want it another way," she says. "Other times you have to put your foot down and stand firm so everything goes right."

Success in this business also comes from taking advantage of every opportunity that comes along. For instance, Loreen had magnetic signs the size of bumper stickers made up that say, "Planning a Wedding?" and that give her web site address. She affixes them to the bumper of her car whenever she goes out for a spin, and at about $20 each, they are a very inexpensive way to advertise her services. Incidentally, she chose to give her internet address instead of her phone number because she thought it would be easier for drivers on the road to remember later.

Loreen also hands out her business card lavishly as a way to generate new leads. "If I go to the bank and the teller is wearing an engagement ring, I give her a card," she says. "I'm always looking at women's left hands."

Finally, patience is a virtue that every consultant we spoke to cited as critical for

Beware!

Don't pretend to be an expert in an area in which you are less experienced or familiar. As always, honesty is the best policy when dealing with your clients. "Your client is paying for professional as well as creative talents. So, if you don't have one of these creative talents, simply say so. You can rely on your well chosen florist or caterer, for instance, to fulfill this need," counsels Robbi Ernst of June Wedding, Inc. Remember, no one person can be a master of all trades!

success. "You have to be patient, both with your clients and your business, because each wedding you're hired for will require different things of you," Lisa M. says.

Nancy Tucker of Coordinators' Corner cracks that being a first-rate wedding consultant means "having the talents of negotiation, mediation, and sometimes levitation!"

And it is exactly that variety, that challenge, and that desire for excellence that makes the wedding consulting business so vital and exciting. May you enjoy great success in your new venture, and may all your dreams and business wishes come true!

Appendix
Wedding Consultant Resources

This appendix is designed to launch your developing wedding consultant business, offering suggestions for everything from certification programs to limousine and disc jockey providers. Although the list is extensive, it is by no means complete. It is one of the wonders of the internet age that at your fingertips, 24/7, you have the virtual world at the ready.

Choose your favorite search engine and start surfing. This is especially important when researching local or regional vendors and associations. Most of the sources listed here are national. You'll want to let your own fingers do the virtual walking when it comes time to finding local sources.

Associations

These groups offer various services and supports to wedding consultants, including, in many cases, professional certification programs.

American Academy of Wedding Professionals, www.aa-wp.com

Association of Bridal Consultants (ABC), (860) 355-0464, www.bridalassn.com

▲

Association of Certified Professional Wedding Consultants (ACPWC), (408) 528-9000, www.acpwc.com

June Wedding, Inc. (JWI), www.junewedding.com

National Bridal Service, (804) 342-0055, www.nationalbridal.com

SuperWeddings.com, www.superweddings.com

Wedding Consultant Certification Institute, www.newbeginningsweddings.com

WeddingSolutions, weddingsolutions.com

Attorney Referrals and Information

Along with these national associations, always check with your state bar association when choosing an attorney.

American Bar Association, www.abanet.org

Find an Attorney, www.findanattorney.com

Lawyers.com, www.lawyers.com

Martindale-Hubbell Law Directory, (800) 526-4902, www.martindale.com

Books

Keep in mind that new books are always being developed and published. Stay up-do-date with regard to what is being published by going online or to your local bookstore. Be sure to check copyright dates when you buy books or check them out from your local library. The wedding consulting field is dynamic and rapidly expanding so books with an older copyright date may not be as useful as newer books.

Amazon, www.amazon.com

Destination Bride, Lisa Light, (F&W Publications, 2005)

The Destination Wedding Workbook, Paris Permenter and John Bigley (booklocker.com, 2004)

Email Marketing: Using Email to Reach Your Target Audience and Build Customer Relationships, Jim Sterne and Anthony Priore (Wiley, 2000)

Great Wedding Tips From the Experts: What Every Bride Can Learn From the Most Successful Wedding Planners, Robbi Ernst III (McGraw-Hill, 2000)

The Portable Wedding Consultant, Leah Ingram (McGraw-Hill, 1997)

Tiffany Wedding, John Loring (1988, Doubleday)

Weddings A-Z, Deborah McCoy and Katharine Dunn (Hay House Lifestyles, 2001)

Weddings by Martha Stewart, Martha Stewart (1987, Clarkson Potter)

Bridal Shows and Information

Many local venues sponsor regional bridal shows. Check with your local chamber of commerce as well as online for shows in your area.

Bridal Association of America, bridalassociationofamerica.com

Bridal Show Producers International, (800) 532-8917, www.bspishows.com

Brides-To-Be, (810) 228-2700, e-mail: info@brides-to-be.com

One Wed, www.onewed.com

Business Software

Of course, there are many, many software applications available, but the big hitters remain QuickBooks Pro, available from Intuit, and Microsoft Office created by Microsoft.

Intuit, intuit.com

Microsoft, microsoft.com

Catering Information

National Association of Catering Executives, www.nace.com

Demographic Information

As you do your market research, these sites will prove valuable.

American Demographics, (212) 210-0100, www.demographics.com

U.S. Census Bureau, www.census.gov

Disc Jockeys

American Disc Jockey Association, (301) 705-5150, www.adja.org

1-800-DISC JOCKEY, www.800dj.com

Employee and Vendor Issues

Better Business Bureau, www.bbb.org

U.S. Department of Labor, www.dol.gov

Flower Information

FTD, www.FTD.com

1800flowers, 1800flowers.com

Limousines

These sources will not only help you to find limousine providers in your area but also help to ensure that you are hiring a reputable firm.

Limos.com, www.limos.com

Limousine Directory, www.limousinedirectory.com

National Limousine Association, www.limo.org

Office Equipment (Phones)

Hello Direct, (800) 444-3556, www.HelloDirect.com

Office Supplies, Forms, and Stationery

With the proliferation of low-cost office supply stores, such as Staples and Office Depot, finding inexpensive office supplies has become a snap.

Mark Art Productions, www.business-stationers.com

Office Depot, www.officedepot.com

Office Max, www.officemax.com

Office Shop Direct, officeshopdirect.com

Overnight Prints, overnightprints.com

Rapidforms, (800) 257-8354, rapidforms.com

Staples, www.staples.com

Online Information Sources

From the most up-to-date statistics to the hottest bridal trends, these are terrific sources.

All Wedding World, allweddingworld.com

Brides, brides.com

The Knot, www.theknot.com

Perfect Wedding Guide, www.perfectweddingguide.com

Premiere Bride, www.premierebride.com

Ultimate Wedding, www.ultimatewedding.com

Wed Alert, wedalert.net

Online Postage

Gone are the days of trudging to the post office for your postage needs. Buy postage or order stamps—even custom-designed stamps—online to be delivered to your front door.

Pitney Bowes, www.pitneyworks.com

Stamps.com, www.stamps.com

USPS, www.usps.com

Zazzle, zazzle.com

Photographer Referrals

Professional Photographers of America Inc., www.ppa.com

Publications

This listing includes both trade and consumer publications that you will find useful.

Advertising Age, www.adage.com

Bridal Guide Magazine, www.bridalguide.com

Bride Again Magazine, www.brideagain.com

Brides, www.brides.com

EXPO, www.expoweb.com

Modern Bride, www.brides.com

Southern Bride, southernbride.com

Today's Bride, www.todaysbrideonline.com

WEDDINGBELLS, www.weddingbells.com

Vows, www.vowsmag.com

Small Business Development Organizations

Along with these national organizations, be sure to check with your local chamber of commerce for help and networking advice as you develop your business.

National Federation of Independent Business, www.NFIB.com

Small Business Administration (SBA), www.sba.gov

Small Business Development Centers (SBDA), www.sba.gov

SCORE, www.score.org

Tax Advice, Help, and Software

H&R Block, www.handrblock.com

Internal Revenue Service, www.irs.ustreas.gov

Intuit TurboTax for Business, www.intuit.com

Trade Show Displays

Airworks Displays & Booths, www.airwork.com

BMA, www.bmadisplay.com

Event Solutions, www.eventsolutions.com

Pinnacle Displays, www.pinnacledisplays.com

New World Case Inc., www.portablebooths.com

Siegel Display Products, www.siegeldisplay.com

SmartExhibits.com, www.smartexhibits.com

Web Hosting

DOMAIN.com, www.domain.com

Prodigy Internet, http://pages.prodigy.net

Webhosting.com, www.webhosting.com

Yahoo!, http://yahoo.com

Wedding Cake Referrals

International Cake Exploration Societé, www.ices.org

Wedding Consultants

Only You, Packy Boukis, JWIC, www.clevelandwedding.com

Dolores Enos, JWIC, www.superweddings.com

June Wedding Inc., Robbi G.W. Ernst III, www.junewedding.com

StarDust Celebrations Inc., Marsha Ballard French, JWIC, and Jenny Cline, JWIC, www.stardustcelebrations.com

Elegant Weddings by Donna, Donna M. Horner, www.elegantweddingsbydonna.com

Studio K, Lisa Kronauer, lkronauer@snet.net

Champagne Taste, Paula Laskelle, www.acpwc.com

American Academy of Wedding Professionals™, Deborah McCoy, www.aa-wp.com

Ever After Weddings, Lisa Michael, JWIC, e-mail: www.junewedding.com

Association of Certified Professional Wedding Consultants, Ann Nola, www.acpwc.com

Coordinators' Corner, Nancy Tucker, www.coordinatorscorner.com

Wedding Planning Software

More general event-planning software is available but these are specifically geared to and designed by wedding consultants.

Event Magic Pro and Room Magic Pro, www.frogwaresoftware.com

Wedding Management for Professionals, www.weddingmanagement.net

Glossary

Backgrounder: a news release that gives general information about your business that will spur the local media to do a more indepth story about your company and services.

Blog: an online newsletter or journal, sometimes with multiple authors.

Brochure: printed sales piece outlining your company's services and capabilities.

CD drive: a device on a computer that plays CDs. It may also be capable of writing to blank CDs.

Central processing unit (CPS): This is a computer's brain. The speed of your CPS is measured in megahertz (MHz) or gigahertz (GHz).

Chat room: on the internet, an electronic "gathering place" for people who share special interests where they can exchange information, comment, or commiserate about topics of mutual interest in real time; see also real time.

Contingency fee: payment for legal services taken as a percentage of a settlement (often 25 percent or higher).

Corporation: a separate legal entity distinct from its owners.

Cyber: related to the internet.

DBA (doing business as): refers to your legal designation once you have selected a business name different from your own and registered it with your local or state government.

Dedicated telephone line: a phone line used for a single purpose, such as for a fax machine or internet data line.

Demographics: the primary characteristics of your target audience, such as age, gender, ethnic background, income level, education level, and home ownership.

Domain name: the address of an internet network (for example, www.entrepreneur.com); see also URL.

DVD drive: a device on your computer that plays DVDs. This drive may also be capable of writing to blank DVDs.

Ergonomic: office furniture or equipment designed for comfort and safety (for example, an ergonomic chair).

Ethernet port: used to connect your computer with the outside world, a port is where you would plug a cable for direct network access.

Executive summary: brief document at the beginning of a report, like a business plan that summarizes its contents.

FAQs: Frequently Asked Questions.

Feature article: an indepth article that tells a story using dialogue, scene-by-scene construction, and personal opinion.

Freelancer: a self-employed person who works on a project or contract basis to produce written materials or artwork for advertisements, brochures, or other printed materials (including news releases).

Gigabyte: a unit of computer memory; most new computer systems now come with 10 gigabytes (or gigs) of memory, which is sufficient to run most business software.

Gutter: in book publishing, the white space formed by adjoining pages of a book when they're bound together.

Hard drive: a computer's permanent storage space.

Hit: in internet parlance, a successful retrieval of information from a web site.

Home page: the gateway to your internet web site.

HTML: Hypertext Markup Language; the coding or computer language used to create web sites.

Icon: a symbol on a web site that links the user to specific information.

Independent contractor: see freelancer.

Interactive: in computer language, characterized by an exchange of data between the computer user and a host like an internet web site.

ISP: Internet Service Provider.

LLC: Limited Liability Company.

Link: a connection on your web site that ties it to another web site.

Litigator: an attorney who represents a client in a lawsuit.

Logo (or logotype): an identifying symbol used by organizations (as in advertising).

Media kit: a packet that contains publicity and sales materials about a company and its services.

Mission statement: a brief summary telling who your company is, what you do, what you stand for, and why you do it.

Modem: Connects your computer to the online network via a phone line; also enables you to send faxes via a phone line.

Navigation: cyber directions given on a web site to help the user to navigate easily from one page to another.

Newsletter: a marketing vehicle that contains short, newsy articles meant to promote a business.

News release: also called "press release"; a one-to-two page article about some positive aspect of your business meant to generate favorable publicity.

Operating system: the program that enables a computer user to tell the computer what to do.

Partnership: a business owned equally by two or more persons, or partners.

Pitch letter: a letter sent to the media to generate interest in your company, product, or service.

Portal: electronic gateways that allow users to "enter" the internet.

Random access memory (RAM): a computer's short-term memory or virtual scratch pad.

Real time: as it happens; in computer lingo, this means you can respond immediately to a message posted on a bulletin board or in a chat room; also known as "instant messaging."

Resolution: the clarity achieved by a printer, scanner, or monitor; measured in dpi (dots per inch).

Retainer: amount of money paid in advance for services.

Rider: an add-on provision to an existing insurance policy designed to protect against losses not covered by the standard policy; homebased wedding consultants typically add general liability and equipment riders to their homeowner's insurance to guard against property loss or injuries to them or their employees on the premises.

SEP (or SEP IRA): Simplified Employee Pension Plan; similar to an IRA, this tax-deferred savings plan has higher contribution limits (15 percent of business income); considered to be a qualified pension plan.

Server: the computer that controls access to a network or peripherals (such as printers or disk drives).

Shareware: software accessible on the internet or on disk that is free of charge or available for a very nominal cost.

Sole proprietorship: a business owned by one person.

Tag line: a slogan used to build audience recognition for a product (i.e., "Got milk?").

Telemarketing: using the telephone to generate new sales or leads.

Thermography: a type of raised printing used on stationery and business cards.

Tussy mussy: a small floral nosegay designed in an antique bouquet holder.

URL: Uniform Resource Locator; or the internet address locator.

Videographer: a person who videotapes an event like a wedding.

Web site: a group of related documents posted in cyberspace, usually accessed through a home page.

Wireless internet card: provides computer network access without a cable.

Index